FINLAND REVEALS HER
SECRET DOCUMENTS

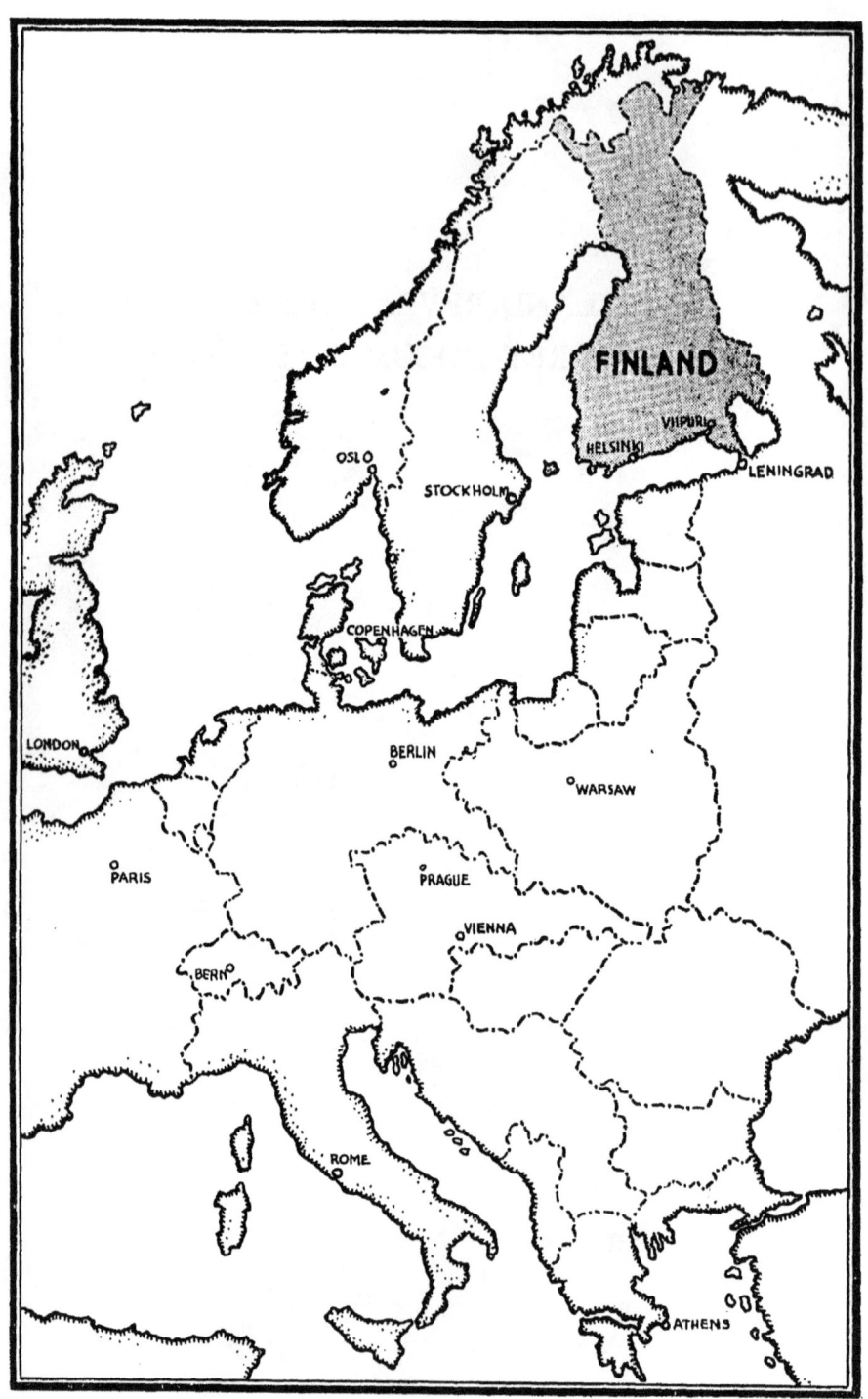

FINLAND'S GEOGRAPHICAL RELATION TO OTHER EUROPEAN COUNTRIES

FINLAND REVEALS HER SECRET DOCUMENTS

ON SOVIET POLICY
MARCH 1940 — JUNE 1941

*The Attitude of the USSR to Finland
after the Peace of Moscow*

WITH A PREFACE BY
HJALMAR J. PROCOPÉ
Minister of Finland to the United States

Publishers
WILFRED FUNK, INC.
New York · 1941

*This title was reproduced in memory of my father, Alvin P. Lind.
A "True Finn" dedicated to his family and "keeping the peace".
Pamela McCallum - Owner, Converpage*

ISBN: 978-0-9835784-8-2
Digitally Reproduced in 2012 by:
Converpage
23 Acorn Street
Scituate, MA 020663
www.converpage.com

PREFACE

THIS book covers a vital period of Finnish-Russian relations, a brief interval between two Russian attacks, between the war ending in March 1940, and the resuming attack in June of this year.

In the Dark Ages the tests of fire and water were often used to weaken the sturdy spirit of those who could not otherwise be subdued. The pages that follow are a record of a new kind of ordeal, an ordeal by peace, imposed by Russia on Finland in the fifteen months following the signing of the Treaty of Moscow, March 12, 1940. The facts, now presented for the first time to the American public, reveal that the Russian policy aimed even in the months of peace at the destruction of Finland's independence.

From the dawn of her history Finland had to defend her soil and her Western way of living against attacks from the East. Out of the past 500 years, one hundred have been for the Finnish nation years of war in defense of home and freedom against the ravaging, destroying and murdering enemy.

Finland held her own. She built her own independent state, the Republic of Finland, and her own life in the orbit of Western, Christian, civilization. In her relations to other nations independent Finland always has had only one aim: to live in peace and peaceful co-operation with other countries. From several years' experience as foreign minister of Finland I can testify that this was the line Finland always most scrupulously followed also in her relations to her big neighbor in the East, to Russia. And Finland thought she would be left in peace. She had taken nothing from anybody and her independence and international status threatened nobody.

Finland was, nevertheless, attacked by Soviet Russia.

All the world now knows what ordeals Finland had to go through less than two years ago. Having taken half of Poland and all the Baltic States Russia turned against Finland. It is obvious what her final aims were: to conquer our country and to introduce Communist rule instead of our age-old democratic political and social system. And behind Finland Russia saw looming the rest of Scandinavia, the rich Swedish and Norwegian mines and the ice-free ports on the Atlantic coast. The fate threatening Finland can be told in one word: annihilation.

In our winter war our friends all over the world gave us their sympathy and support. President Roosevelt's words in a speech in February, 1940, when he said that American sympathy was 98 per cent with the Finns and that this sympathy was axiomatic, constituted strong encouragement to the Finnish people fighting for their lives and freedom.

We received much diversified help during our struggle in the winter 1939/40, but we did not get from anywhere what would have been absolutely essential—military assistance. We had to fight alone against odds of 50 to 1 and finally we had to make peace on the fateful 12th of March 1940.

The Treaty of Peace that Russia imposed upon Finland was a hard one, taking from us 10 per cent of our territory, since time immemorial old Finnish soil, including 12 per cent of our country's wealth: land, water-power, forests, farms and factories. Finland was bleeding and suffering and, furthermore, threatened by famine and exposure. An official American Red Cross investigation has shown that during much of the period covered in this book Finland had, as she still has, to survive on only about half of the food considered the minimum necessary.

But Finland did not despair. With firm determination the Finnish nation took up the task of reconstruction and rehabilitation. Her efforts were this time directed towards reconstruction, not towards revenge. Even though the stipulations of the Peace Treaty were hard, the people of Finland accepted them without reservation. In a speech, partly quoted in this book, Mr. Risto Ryti, President of Finland, recently explained our country's policy in the following way:

"Accustomed to keep its word, the Finnish nation wished to honour the agreements we were compelled to conclude in Moscow. In our hearts we decided, and also declared on innumerable occasions, that we had to regain all that was lost in Carelia by domestic reforms and new productive work within our new frontiers. Cold deliberation brought us to that conclusion. The idea of revenge has not appeared and has not influenced our policy. On the Finnish side we tried to forget the wrongs and humiliations inflicted on us; although the wounds struck by the Soviet Union's war of aggression, begun in defiance of all international justice and moral principles, burned in the hearts of the entire nation. The point from which we set out was, that seeing we had to live in this corner of the world, from generation to generation, in the immediate neighborhood of Russia, our relations with that country had to be organized. In spite of all that had happened, we wished to build up a lasting peace with the Soviet Union."

But Russia never intended to allow Finland to build a lasting peace. It is now known to all the world that the Soviet Prime Minister Molotov last November stated in Berlin the Russian communist government's intention to strike a final blow at Finland and liquidate her.

The fifteen months of so-called peace was for Finland a long road to Golgotha, of which the world knew little.

Finland could not appeal to world opinion. Had she done so, her relations to Russia would only have further deteriorated, endangering still more the peace Finland was determined to maintain.

Stripped of its trappings there is presented in this book a picture of a big, burly and uncompromisingly belligerent neighbor ceaselessly outraging the little fellow next door. We find nearly every transgression possible during the so-called state of peace between the two nations, from the unsuccessful attempt to create a fifth column and the time-worn subterfuge of increasing consular staffs in order to build up personnel for a spy system, to outright and outrageous demands for territorial privileges, for concessions already granted another state and in addition violations of territorial and national integrity for which there are few parallels in history. Some of them, such as the demand that their diplomats be permitted transport in Soviet submarines, seem even ludicrous.

Americans will see in this book examples of Finland's firm belief in granted rights, her own and other peoples'. Herein is described how for months on end Finland resisted Russia's demands to cancel a contract with an Anglo-American company, even in the face of the most severe Russian threats and of Russia's withholding thousands of tons of promised and desperately needed grain in an effort to force Finland to hand over to the communists this foreign property.

The reader will find how Russia forced Finland to allow the transport of Russian troops through the southern part of the country. Only after this agreement was forced on Finland the transit of German troops through northern Finland to and from Norway was granted. The German transit has been played up in the world press; the Russian transit has scarcely been mentioned although the Russian troops passed right through the heart of the southern part of our country, while the Germans went mainly through the wilderness of Lapland.

This book shows how Soviet troops in the border regions and Russian airplanes again and again violated Finnish territory and how Finland lived under a constant threat of a renewal of the attack that failed to destroy her liberty in 1940.

Because of the unremitting severity of Russia's ordeal by peace, people may feel that Finland, however justly, might have taken up arms against Russia on June 26th in a spirit of revenge. Many Americans have told me that they were glad that Finland was going to get a chance to avenge herself. But nothing could be further from the truth as to the way that Finland was forced into the present conflict. Finland wanted only peace and an opportunity to rebuild her country.

In the morning of June 22nd, only a couple of hours after the Russian-German hostilities had broken out, Russia began to bomb and shell peaceful Finnish territory, perhaps in the false hope that Finnish morale would break and Finland would let in the Russian troops. But even then Finland did not take up arms. Although the Russian attacks were directed chiefly against fully open localities and the civilian population, Finland did not counter-attack. She protested through diplomatic channels, but got no answer to her representations. Finally, on the 25th of June, the Soviet forces launched a general attack upon the country, through regular and extensive hostilities in all parts of Finland, waging war and resuming the aggression of 1939. Only then, when Russia had openly resorted to war, did Finland decide to use all military force at her command in order to defend her country and her people. Thus Finland did not begin this war. She was forced to defend herself, she had no choice.

Finland's position today has been fully and frankly stated by President Ryti: "The world must understand that Finland is fighting this war only against Russia; we are not parties in the big European struggle." Getting help from the only quarter that could and would help her in her present deadly struggle into which she has been forced by the communist aggression, Finland is fighting for her liberty, her security, and the right to her place in the world, free from constant threat. As President Ryti so cogently said only a few days ago: "In a single word, 'security,' one might contemplate all our interests."

We still believe in peaceful co-operation between nations. The record of the documents in this book prove as clearly as anything the need for a firm international order, based upon right and justice—one which will grant also small nations real and lasting security.

We Finns will not give up our free way of living; we will live also in the future as our ancestors did, as free men in a free country. For this we fight and for this the whole Finnish nation, from the labor unions and the social democratic party to the right wing groups, stand united today as yesterday and forever. There can be no compromise about freedom in Finland.

Thus, standing up against the communist aggression that now threatens her, fighting for her very existence, for her homes, for her Christian faith and her free way of living, the Finnish nation feels that she fulfills her duty not only towards herself but also towards the civilization to which she belongs.

The relations between Finland and the United States have been of the very best during all the time that Finland has existed as an independent state. To America Finland has deep gratitude. America lent her the money which helped to avert widespread starvation in 1919. Finland got assistance from her in different ways during these last hard and difficult years. America has often expressed her sympathy and understanding for the Finns' efforts to live in peace and freedom. I hope that the publication of the documents in this book will contribute toward preserving and promoting the understanding and sympathy for Finland in the United States.

HJALMAR J. PROCOPÉ

Washington, D. C.
August 1941.

CONTENTS

CHAPTER	PAGE
INTRODUCTION	xi
I. Difficulties in the Execution of the Peace Treaty, and the Unwillingness of the USSR to Enter into Normal Relations with Finland	1
II. Peace without Security	6
III. Russian Interference in the Domestic Affairs of Finland	15
IV. Russian Extortion of Special Rights and Concessions	18
V. Trade between Finland and the USSR, 1940–1941	29
VI. Violations of Finnish Territory by the USSR	31
VII. Policy of Pressure Ends in Attack	33
Treaty of Peace between the Republic of Finland and the Union of Soviet Socialist Republics.	
Documents, 1–74	40
Index	107

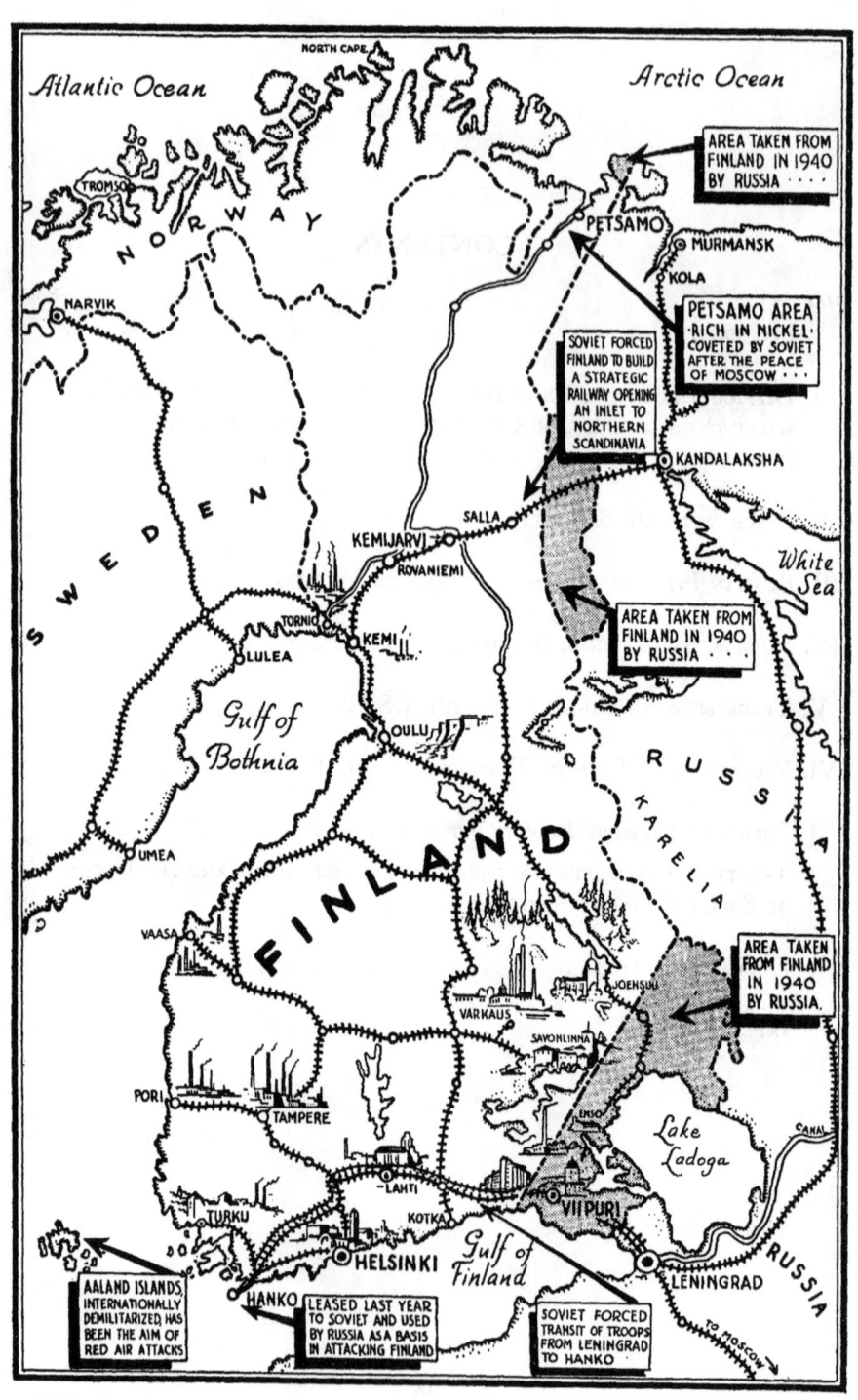

THE TREND OF THE SOVIET POLICY TOWARD THE ATLANTIC OCEAN

INTRODUCTION

Soon after the conclusion of the Peace of Moscow, it became apparent that the Government of the USSR had no intention to apply loyally the principle of good neighborly relations enunciated in the Peace Treaty. Disconcerting incidents had already occurred during the preliminary demarcation of the new boundary. The only explanation was that the USSR Government intentionally exceeded its rights under the Peace Treaty, and strove to act as a victor and conqueror who could afford to ignore the rights of the other party to the treaty.

During the peace negotiations the Soviet delegates declared that their demands were dictated by military considerations, that the new frontier had been defined accordingly, and that in the demarcation and detailed delimitation of the frontier the USSR had no intention of obtaining economic advantages from Finland. Nevertheless, in connection with the actual delimitation of the new frontier line, the USSR uncompromisingly demanded the Enso industrial area.

Later, in the course of 1940, the attitude of the USSR Government brought it to a point where it proceeded directly to interfere with the purely domestic affairs of Finland. Thus it lent support, through diplomatic channels, to activities pursued in Finland by a revolutionary group bent on fostering disorder. These activities stemmed from agitation directed from Soviet quarters, and were carried out by their agents.

The same imperialistic intention of the USSR Government to obtain power of fiat in Finland was likewise disclosed by certain concrete questions between the two States. Soviet demands in connection with these questions went far beyond the limits of the Peace Treaty, which, according to Soviet Government assurances, would completely satisfy the claims of the USSR on Finland. This was true of the question of transit traffic on Hanko, of the demilitarization of the Aaland Islands, of the right to exploit the Petsamo nickel mines, and of certain other matters. Some of these questions were settled in the autumn of 1940 in accordance with Soviet demands, because Finland, while attempting to defend her rights against each new demand by persistent negotiation and step-by-step retreat, ultimately had no choice in the circumstances but to go as far as possible toward meeting these demands. However, this did not check, in the slightest degree, the extremely malevolent radio and press campaign and agitation directed against Finland from the USSR, nor did it change the exacting and arrogant attitude of the official Soviet representatives to the Finnish authorities.

For her part Finland had tried, after the conclusion of the peace, to fulfill honestly and scrupulously her treaty obligations to the USSR, and in every respect to maintain good neighborly relations (Document 25). With a view to consolidating peaceful relations the Finnish Government sincerely endeavored, apart from purely political relations, to find means for establishing a better understanding and mutually profitable contacts with Soviet circles in various spheres of life (trade, culture, etc.). These Finnish efforts, however, were treated with complete disdain in Soviet quarters. It became obvious that the USSR, except for the political relations between the two governments, wished to be in contact solely with subversive Finnish elements. In the economic sphere the USSR finally resorted to a direct trade war on Finland.

All this, in the light of what had befallen the Baltic States, left no doubt whatever in the minds of those responsible for Finnish foreign policy as to the ultimate aims of USSR policy in regard to Finland. That the USSR Government aimed from the very beginning at eventual military conquest of Finland, is shown by certain circumstances connected with the provisions of the Treaty of Moscow. The line of the new frontier was fixed so as to weaken Finland's possibilities of defense and to place the USSR in a more advantageous offensive position than before the war. At the Moscow peace negotiations, demands were unexpectedly made for the cession of territories in northeast Finland and the construction of the Salla railway, which were not included in the original demands submitted to the Finnish Government. From the point of view of an offensive, the strategic significance of these new demands, clearly directed against northern Scandinavia as well as Finland, was obvious.

The aims of the USSR in regard to Finland found a striking expression during the visit of Commissar for Foreign Affairs Molotov to Berlin in November, 1940. In the course of the negotiations in Berlin, M. Molotov proposed that the USSR should be allowed to attack Finland a second time, without interference by Germany.

In the early spring of 1941, Soviet pressure became somewhat weaker, to be sure. The reason was not, however, that the USSR, on its own initiative, had begun to strive for real co-operation with Finland. On the contrary, the Moscow Government continued, though in less aggressive form, to maintain its unreasonable attitude. This was true, for instance, in the question of the nickel mines. Unjustifiable demands were made and unfounded objections raised in connection with transit traffic on Hanko. Other similar recent illustrations prove that the USSR Government in fact continued its attempts to dictate directives to Finland, and that it had by no means abandoned is original intentions regarding that country.

The change of tone that was ascertainable in the Soviet Government's behavior must be attributed to the changes which had occurred in the balance of power on the European continent. These changes had shaken the dominating position of the USSR in eastern Europe.

In the following chapters, Finnish-Soviet relations are detailed. They elucidate the various questions that rose between Finland and the USSR. The picture which these accounts provide reveals with all possible clarity that the design of the USSR was gradually to reduce Finland, by persistent and unlimited demands, to a state of enslavement, until the nation became ripe for submission to the political overlordship of Moscow, or, if this failed, to embark on a new invasion of Finland.

CHAPTER I

DIFFICULTIES IN THE EXECUTION OF THE PEACE TREATY, AND THE UNWILLINGNESS OF THE USSR TO ENTER INTO NORMAL RELATIONS WITH FINLAND

The Peace of Moscow was hastily concluded on March 12, 1940, while military operations were in full swing, the USSR refusing to consent to an armistice for the period of the negotiations. During the conclusion of peace, Russian demands were unexpectedly presented for the cession of territory in northeast Finland and for the construction of the Salla railway. These demands had not been included in the preliminary peace terms communicated to the Finnish Government. Furthermore, the preliminary peace terms were vague in that the Finnish Government had not been given to understand that the cession of the whole of Viipuri Bay and of the Ladoga coast to the USSR was intended. The USSR dictated a peace which Finland was compelled to accept. In the circumstances one would have thought that the Peace Treaty satisfied the USSR, and that Finland would now be left in peace, as indeed the Soviet Government had said would be the case (cf. Documents 5-6). This did not come to pass, however.

Already in the execution of the Peace Treaty initial difficulties were encountered which revealed that the Soviet Government was determined not merely to extract the greatest possible advantage from the treaty, but arbitrarily to go farther than the treaty justified.

1. In certain sectors of the frontier, Soviet forces conspicuously disregarded the time schedules (fixed in the protocol appended to the Peace Treaty) according to which they were to advance. The result was that the evacuation permitted under the treaty was prevented. Instead of indemnifying persons moving out of those areas for the loss caused by this breach of the treaty, the USSR did not even consent to the transfer into Finland of privately owned fodder, stocks of grain, and agricultural machinery which had been left near the new frontier.

2. Having thus advanced in a manner contrary to agreement, the Russians seized and detained, near the border, several members of the Finnish Army and civilians, who were not shown to have crossed the frontier at all, or who had crossed the frontier by mistake while it was still undelimited and indeterminate. In spite of repeated requests and proposals for an arrangement, the

USSR did not consent to repatriate them, although Finland sent back several USSR nationals who had crossed the border into Finland during the summer of 1940. When M. Molotov was approached on the subject, he merely accused the Finns of espionage and used threatening language.

3. In the demarcation of the new boundary, the USSR, at the sessions of the Mixed Frontier Commission, arbitrarily interpreted the frontier line marked on the map appended to the Peace Treaty in such a manner as to leave Enso [1] on the USSR side. When Finland took up the question of Enso through diplomatic channels, Molotov simply pointed to Enso on a map which was before him and declared emphatically that little hills might be discussed, but not Enso, for Enso was Russia's. Later the USSR demanded the Pelkola Estate, located near Enso; the question of compensation to Finland was treated by the USSR as an unimportant side-issue. The USSR refused to listen to well-grounded Finnish proposals (the shifting of the frontier to a point more favorable for the floating of timber on the River Koitajoki,[2] the transfer to Finland of timber left behind in the Enso area), but finally consented for form's sake to a minor frontier revision in an area relatively insignificant from an economic point of view.

4. At the request of the Soviet authorities, an engineer and technical staff remained to operate the Rouhiala power plant,[3] which passed to the USSR under the terms of the Peace Treaty. These persons were not permitted to leave after a reasonable period. They were detained at the power station by semicompulsory methods and were not paid the remuneration promised them for their work. On the other hand, the USSR demanded an exorbitant price for the electrical power supplied at the time to Finland from the Rouhiala plant and refused to consider a reduction.

5. When the Peace Treaty went into effect, the Dorpat Peace Treaty of 1920 and agreements based on it became invalid. The Moscow Peace Treaty had been drafted in such haste that—in spite of the efforts of the Finnish delegates—provisions pertaining even to matters of first-class importance were not included. Soviet quarters pointed out that such matters could be settled later through diplomatic channels. Afterwards, however, the USSR adopted a passive or a negative attitude in regard to the settlement of questions which did not primarily affect its own interests, although during the negotiations it had intimated its willingness to conclude separate agreements with reference to questions mentioned in Paragraphs (f) and (g) below.

---

[1] *Enso* is a center of the woodworking industry in the Vuoksi Valley, owned by the Enso-Gutzeit Company. It comprises large modern sulphate, sulphite and board mills. An isinglass factory was situated on the Pelkola Estate belonging to the Enso-Gutzeit Company.

[2] *Koitajoki*. A river flowing from the Russian frontier through the Ilomantsi rural commune; of some importance as a floating channel for timber. Under the Moscow Treaty part of the river came into the possession of the USSR, with the result that this old floating channel was blocked.

[3] *Rouhiala*. A new power plant on the Vuoksi River about 10 kilometers below the Enso factories. The plant, completed in 1937, is situated in the Jaaski rural commune.

(a) Thus, the USSR did not consent to the organization of option rights for the population of the ceded territory, or to guarantee the rights of inhabitants who remained in the ceded areas. The USSR did, however, permit the inhabitants of the Hyrsyla district,[4] who were left there when hostilities broke out, to return to Finland. A Finnish proposal that persons who had been induced by an energetic Russian radio propaganda during the world depression after 1929 to enter the USSR, could return to Finland, was rejected by the USSR. The USSR declared that such matters were its own domestic concern.

(b) A proposal by Finland that she should be allowed to utilize the Saimaa Canal[5] for the passage of merchant vessels and Uuras[6] as a loading site was rejected by the USSR. A new proposal for a temporary arrangement of this kind to be in force up to the end of 1940 was similarly rejected by the USSR because of opposition in Soviet military quarters.

(c) The lease of the Hanko area placed obstacles in the way of Finnish coastal traffic. Finland consequently proposed that the USSR should grant merchant vessels free passage through the waters of the leased area. The USSR refused its consent.

(d) The USSR would not agree to joint arrangements of fishery rights in the Arctic Ocean and the Gulf of Finland, although on the latter point the USSR had intimated earlier that it viewed the matter favorably. As regards fishery rights in the Arctic Ocean, the USSR referred to the absence in the Peace Treaty of any basis for discussions on this point, although during the negotiations for the treaty the Russians had expressly declared that "details" could be dealt with later.

(e) The USSR has not consented to conclude the timber-floating agreement made necessary by the changes caused in the floating channels in the frontier area by the new political frontier, although the question was one of joint floating channels. Its explanation was a brief remark to the effect that the matter aroused no interest in Soviet economic circles. Before 1939, however, when the frontier followed a more natural course, a floating agreement was in existence.

(f) Representations have frequently been made by Finland regarding

---

[4] *Hyrsyla.* A sack-like bulge on the eastern frontier in the Suojarvi rural commune, the inhabitants of which could not be evacuated in time before the arrival of Soviet troops. They were transferred to the USSR for the period of the war, and were not allowed to return to Finland until after the conclusion of peace. The population of the territory ceded to the USSR under the terms of the Peace Treaty, altogether about half a million people, voluntarily moved with scarcely an exception to localities situated farther west.

[5] *Saimaa Canal.* A canal about 58 kilometers long from Lake Saimaa to Viipuri linking Lake Saimaa and through that the entire waterway system of East Finland with the Gulf of Finland. The frontier imposed by the Moscow Peace Treaty cuts the canal in two.

[6] *Uuras.* Outer harbor of Viipuri, situated about 12 kilometers distant from that city at the mouth of Viipuri Bay. Uuras has been of great importance, particularly as a loading place for timber.

the return of archives which were left in ceded territory. At first, the USSR intimated that it viewed the matter favorably. Attempts to bring about an arrangement have meanwhile been fruitless, because of the passive attitude of the USSR.

(g) Attempts were made by Finland to restore normal peace-time conditions on the new political frontier based on a treaty agreement. For this purpose Finland presented to the USSR a draft treaty relative to the settlement of possible border incidents and the prevention of border disputes. The Soviet Government took the matter under consideration and promised to submit its own counterproposals. After the elapse of many months this had still not arrived.

6. While the USSR has been unwilling to help in the restoration to Finland of very important archive material which is of no significance to the USSR, the USSR has regarded it as natural and self-evident that Finland should surrender various scientific and other material relating to the ceded territory.

On several occasions the USSR requested Finland to provide various kinds of scientific and technical material concerning the ceded territory. On these occasions, reference was simply made to the circumstance that the territory had been transferred to the USSR under the terms of the Peace Treaty; sometimes it was declared outright that Russia was entitled to this material. As Finland did not desire to arouse ill-will toward itself, Finland in general consented to provide materials which were not very important, although their compilation had meant considerable expenditure of effort. For instance, the Soviet Government was furnished with specially extensive meteorological, hydrological, hydrographical, and geological data relating to the ceded territory and the leased Hanko area. The USSR also requested that it should be regularly furnished with hydrological and meteorological information concerning Lake Saimaa and the River Vuoksi. Finland felt that these requests also could be met within certain limits, but practical arrangements were still incomplete when the new attack on Finland was launched in June, 1941. By request of the USSR, plans of the technical plant and of the towns in the ceded territory and Hanko were also provided.

7. Under the terms of the Peace Treaty, Finland was to construct, if possible, her section of the Kemijarvi-Kandalaksha Railway (the so-called Salla railway) before the end of 1940. The amount of labor involved in the construction of this railway, difficulties of supply arising out of the present exceptional circumstances, Arctic climatic conditions, and other reasons made the completion of the railway impossible during 1940. The Soviet Government, however, showed no understanding whatever of the explanations, supported by facts, which the Finnish Government presented, but instead only impatience and suspicion. Greater speed was urged on several occasions in the construction

work, and Finland was unjustly accused of holding up the work. When the Finnish delegates pointed out, during the Moscow peace negotiations, that Finland suffered from a shortage of rails and bridge building materials, and that this circumstance alone would prevent the completion of the railway in 1940, M. Molotov declared that the USSR was prepared to place at Finland's disposal the rails and bridge-building materials the Finns thought they would require. A request was subsequently forwarded from Finland for specified quantities of material to be used for the purpose, but the USSR never even troubled to reply. Instead, the Soviet Minister to Finland, M. Zotov, found it appropriate at the end of 1940 to go so far as to set the date by which the railway would have to be finished, and to express the opinion that unless this date was observed, the Soviet Government would regard Finland's behavior as being in conflict with the Peace Treaty. The pressure exerted by him in Helsinki was followed shortly afterwards in Moscow by pressure brought to bear on M. Paasikivi, Finland's Minister to the USSR, by the Commissariat for Foreign Affairs. Before that date Finland had already promised the USSR that the railway would be completed by the autumn of 1941. (Documents 49, 55, and 57.)

CHAPTER II

PEACE WITHOUT SECURITY

IN THE spring of 1940 it became evident in various ways that the USSR intended to use the Peace Treaty as a means of extorting further concessions from Finland. The arbitrary manner in which the USSR interpreted the Peace Treaty greatly reduced the security which the treaty assured Finland. Under the cover of the Peace Treaty the USSR considered it appropriate to impose entirely new demands on Finland. The demands related to Finnish foreign policy, to new concessions sought by the Soviet, and to Finnish domestic affairs.

1. Prevention of a Northern Defensive Alliance

The first demand based on an arbitrary interpretation of the Peace Treaty concerned Finnish foreign policy. In that treaty each signatory undertook to refrain from all attacks on the other, and agreed not to enter into any alliance or coalition aimed at the other contracting party (Article 3). Appealing to this part of the treaty, the USSR took a decisive stand against the defensive alliance which was being planned between Finland and the other northern countries at the time peace was being negotiated. Yet the contemplated defensive alliance (if only because of the neutral policy Sweden and Norway were persistently pursuing) could in no way be regarded as embodying the idea of revenge on the USSR (Documents 1-7).

The USSR made no attempt whatever to investigate the character of this agreement, which had not got past the preliminary drafting stage, but regarded itself as competent, on the grounds of the Peace Treaty, to prevent its realization. This proved a definite attempt on the part of the USSR to dominate Finnish foreign policy, though the effort was cloaked by the pretense of seeking moral justification for it in the Peace Treaty.

In the autumn of 1940 the USSR returned to the subject of the defensive alliance, obstinately alleging that a "conspiracy" was being hatched between Finland and Sweden (Documents 28, 30, and 33). All that was involved, however, was an attempt to bring about closer northern co-operation, this time, naturally, with Sweden alone.

On Finnish Independence Day, December 6, 1940, M. Molotov presented to M. Paasikivi a document in which it was alleged, on the basis of reports from the Soviet Minister in Stockholm, Madame Kollontay, that an agreement was being drafted between Finland and Sweden which would place Finnish foreign policy under the control of Stockholm. Finland was advised to consider the consequences of such an agreement between Finland and any foreign power, not excepting Sweden. M. Molotov returned to the subject again on December 18 (Documents 50, 53, 54, and 56).

2. *Demands for Restoration of and Compensation for Property in Southeast Finland*

Restoration of Property

In the middle of April, 1940, M. Molotov addressed complaints to M. Paasikivi about the removal of property belonging to industrial establishments in the territory ceded to Russia. As the USSR was of the opinion that the removal had taken place contrary to Article 6 of the Protocol appended to the Peace Treaty, it called on Finland to restore and compensate for such property. Finland promised, in the very first answer given to this complaint, to fulfill this demand in the case of any industrial plant which had been removed or damaged after the conclusion of peace. At the same time, the charges made by the USSR which referred to concrete cases, were answered point by point. It was possible to establish that the complaints were for the most part unfounded, and that they partly referred to industrial plants situated in territory already occupied by Soviet forces when peace was made.

The USSR soon made a political dispute of the matter by accusing Finland, in a long and sharply worded article in the *Pravda* on May 7, 1940, of a breach of the Peace Treaty. M. Paasikivi therefore sent a letter on the subject that same day to the editor of the *Pravda* (Document 8) which was published on May 8, 1940. The Leningrad broadcasting station also took up the matter in an accusing tone (Document 9).

Because of these accusations Finland presented, on May 10, 1940, a proposal for the appointment of a Mixed Committee of Investigation, to which the USSR consented on May 11. The first meeting of the committee, on May 23, revealed a fundamental divergence of views regarding the interpretation of Article 6 of the Protocol. Finland argued that no liability could exist concerning property removed or destroyed while hostilities were still in progress, or, in other words, prior to eleven o'clock on March 13. But the USSR demanded the return of all property, and compensation for property and plant destroyed, irrespective of the date of the removal or destruction. Russia refused to accept the Finnish explanation that as a precautionary measure valuable machinery had naturally been moved during the war into the interior from the vicinity of the frontier. It contended that the greater part of the removals and destruction had taken place after the conclusion of peace, and that it was up to Finland to furnish the proof to the contrary.

Finland endeavored to reach clarity in the matter also through diplomatic channels. The Commissariat for Foreign Affairs, however, obstructed these endeavors by postponing the reception of M. Paasikivi by about ten days. Finally, on June 8, he was able to take the matter up with Assistant Commissar for Foreign Affairs Dekanosov, to whom he presented a memorandum (Document 11) on Finland's standpoint and proposals. M. Dekanosov stated that he rejected the Finnish standpoint and regarded Article 6 of the Protocol as implying that the military command of each party engaged to undertake measures for restoring and putting into operation destroyed or removed establishments.

An attempt by Finland to reach a definitive settlement in the matter by consenting to restore the entire plant of the Enso group of factories, irrespective of the date when removal took place, also failed. In return for this concession, to be sure, the Soviet delegates in the Mixed Committee were induced to promise that Finland would be indemnified for property removed during the war and subsequently restored, but they were not persuaded to refrain from further demands.

The Soviet delegates brought pressure to bear on Finland for this concession by hinting that unless Finland agreed to it at once, as a preliminary condition, the demand for compensation for property destroyed would be vastly greater than the value of the property removed. They gave the Finnish delegates to understand that in return for the surrender of the Enso machinery the demand for compensation might be reduced. Further, the USSR systematically kept Finland, at this stage of the negotiations as well as later, in ignorance of the extent of its demands.

In the circumstances Finland had no choice, faced as she was with the threat of strained relations which in the prevailing situation would have been a grave matter, but to submit to the USSR's demands, meanwhile adhering to her standpoint in principle and repeatedly reaffirming it during the negotiations.

The only concession which the USSR was induced to make was the promise to credit Finland, in the compensation account payable for destroyed property, for the restoration of property removed while the war was still in progress. In spite of this, however, the USSR tenaciously adhered to the principle that Finland was liable for restoring even property coming under this heading. This is evident, not only from the discussions in the Mixed Committee, but from the circumstance that any property removed before the peace, which for various reasons could not be restored, was forthwith included in the calculations presented to Finland by the Soviet delegates as property for which Finland would have to pay compensation. At one stage the USSR tightened the noose by threatening to demand compensation for the losses suffered by the factories while they had been shut down, if restoration were not effected with the utmost speed.

Later, new demands were added in the handling of the question of restoration. In most cases Finland was compelled to accept them. Thus, in the course of the negotiations, the USSR on several occasions added to and expanded its lists of demands in respect of different factories. It also demanded, in several instances, the surrender of stocks of spare parts and raw materials in quantities which, in the opinion of the USSR, well-equipped factories should possess, regardless of whether or not the factories in question had maintained any such stocks before the war. Finland had actually to order machinery and equipment for the USSR from abroad to replace machinery and equipment removed during or even before the war. The building and machinery plans of many of the factories had also to be surrendered. Finland refused, however, to surrender the working and machinery plans of the Waldhof Company's plant, as well as the patents and licenses utilized by the Kuitu Rayon Company, because of existing obligations entered into with interests abroad which involved property rights. The USSR also interpreted the term "economic institutions" in the widest possible sense to cover moving-picture theaters, small sawmills for domestic needs, nature-cure sanatoria, fishermen's motorboats, etc. It was not until Finland had pointed out the absurdities to which such demands led in practice, that the USSR abandoned some of them.

The economic values involved in the Soviet demands may be seen from the following list of the most important industrial establishments for which Finland was compelled to surrender or restore machinery and other property: The Enso-Gutzeit Oy. sulphite and sulphate cellulose and board mills at Enso; the Kuitu Oy. artificial wool and rayon factory; the Oy. Waldhof Ab, cellulose mills; the Karelia Wood Oy. plywood factory at Hamekoski; the Ladoga Timber Oy. plywood factory at Lahdenpohja; the Hame Faneeritehdas Oy. plywood factory in Sortavala; the Helyla joinery works; the Enso joinery works; the Kakisalmen Saha Oy. and Laatokan Saha Oy. sawmills; the Laskelan Saha sawmill; the Torajarven Saha Oy. sawmill; the Inkilan Saha Oy. sawmill; the Itasuomen Raakasokeritehdas Oy. sugar factory at Antrea; the Wartsila Company's iron mills at Wartsila; the Hamekoski Smelting Works; the Sortavalan Telakka ja Konepaja Oy. shipyard and machine shop; the Liljeqvistin Konepaja Oy. machine shop in Kakisalmi; the Co-operative Wholesale Society, S.O.K. flour mills in Viipuri; the Consumers' Co-operative Wholesale Society, OTK flour mills in Jaaski; the Ruskeala marble quarry; the Hamekoski power plant; the Rouhiala Oy. power plant. Among the smaller enterprises might be mentioned eight other power plants, eleven co-operative dairies, electric current transformers, power motors, a couple of printing establishments, brick factories, etc.

In addition, Finland surrendered, at the demand of the USSR, railway rolling stock comprising 75 locomotives, 120 passenger coaches, and 1,868 freight cars, spare parts for these, railway station equipment including telephone and telegraph equipment, fittings and building appliances belonging to the Saimaa Canal, the fittings and equipment of local post offices and telephone exchanges, motor cars, trucks and motorized fire-fighting apparatus, the plant of the Sortavala broadcasting station, certain tugs and lighters, etc.

Compensation for Destruction

The Russian demand for compensation for destroyed property was brought forward at the very start of the discussions. Finnish explanations that the destruction had been caused partly by aerial bombardment and other acts of war, even as late as the last night of hostilities before the news of the signature of the Peace Treaty had reached the responsible authorities, were disregarded.

Then, while negotiations were proceeding for the restoration of property, the USSR abstained from bringing up the question of compensation for destroyed property. But by occasional vague hints and by keeping Finland in ignorance of the extent of the compensation demanded, the Soviet Government utilized the issue as an instrument of extortion in its demands for restoration.

It was not until the end of November 1940, after the demands for restoration of property had been dealt with almost in their entirety, that the Soviet delegation again took up the question of compensation for property that had been destroyed. The total claim presented by it was roughly 145 million roubles (about 1,800 million Finnish marks or an equivalent of $36,000,000), from which amount, however, the delegation "felt that it could" make certain deductions. On the grounds of the promise of indemnification referred to earlier and, according to its own statement "on its own responsibility and without the permission of the Soviet Government," the delegation reduced its final demand to approximately 95 million roubles, viz. 1,200 million marks or about $24,000,000, to be paid within six months. In answer to the Finnish expressions of surprise at the size of the claim and the basis on which it was calculated, the Soviet delegates remarked that the claim was not a war indemnity and that it fell far short of meeting the cost of reconstruction work in Karelia.

In a reply presented on January 8, 1941, Finland refused to accept either the Soviet standpoint in regard to Finland's liability to pay compensation or the basis on which the claim presented had been calculated. Finland declared that she adhered to her standpoint that she was liable only for destruction carried out after eleven o'clock on March 13, 1940. In conformity with this principle, and by a liberal application of it, Finland regarded herself as liable for damage estimated at a little more than 8 million roubles only, or about $2,000,000, and repudiated the USSR claim in excess of that figure. On the other hand, the indemnification due to Finland for the restoration of machinery was estimated, according to careful Finnish calculations, at roughly

46 million roubles, or about $11,500,000. Finland thus had a claim against the USSR amounting to the difference between the two figures.

Although the USSR made no attempt, after the receipt of this answer, to return to the question of compensation, it had become obvious during the negotiations that it would be impossible to obtain a reduction of the Soviet demand by reasoned arguments or exhaustive and detailed explanations. The negotiations left the impression that the USSR had begun by fixing the approximate size of the compensation it would demand, and then drafted bases of calculation which led to the figure chosen. In this connection it is worth recalling that during the peace negotiations M. Molotov twice used the term war "indemnity," and pointed out how nobly the USSR was acting in not imposing any war indemnity on Finland.

3. *Demands for Restoration of Property in the Hanko Area*

In a memorandum presented to M. Paasikivi (Document 10) on June 2, 1940, the USSR demanded—on the initiative, it is believed, of the Soviet Minister in Helsinki, M. Zotov—the restoration also of the property removed from the Hanko area which had been leased to Russia. The USSR based this arbitrary demand on Article 4 of the Peace Treaty, and not on Article 6 of the Protocol, as in the case of southeast Finland. By way of reply, Finland stated in a well-reasoned factual memorandum of June 10 (Document 12), that in her view no liability rested on her under the Peace Treaty, and declared that the evacuation had been carried out in good faith.

The matter was investigated in Moscow for some weeks, after which the USSR, in a memorandum presented on July 6 (Document 17) repeated the demand for the return of all military and civilian property removed from Hanko.

In the existing situation Finland regarded it as impossible to delay a solution of the problem. The Mixed Committee was, therefore, entrusted with negotiating and drafting a proposal for the settlement of the matter in conformity with principles agreed upon in advance by an exchange of memoranda (Documents 20 and 21) in the Committee. In the Finnish memorandum it was again emphasized that Finland was under no obligation to return the property in question, but actually the memorandum contained an acceptance of the heavy Soviet demands. For this reason the USSR accepted the proposed suggestion for a settlement.

During the negotiations in the Mixed Committee the USSR nevertheless again attempted to tighten its grip and demanded, in disregard of the principles agreed upon, the restoration of all private property as well. Finland succeeded, however, in parrying this demand.

Both Governments then accepted the settlement drafted in October (Document 35), which was based on the terms agreed upon in the memorandum.

According to the October agreement, public property was to be returned. Finland was to pay cash compensation for defensive equipment, with no obligation to return it in kind. Private property was not to be returned, except in a few special cases. In addition to the restoration of property agreed upon, Finland had later to furnish Hanko, for the benefit of the USSR, with railway rolling stock and property taken away during the evacuation from private houses, such as bathtubs, linoleum floor covering, etc.

4. *Difficulties Arising out of the Russian Consulate in Petsamo*

Article 6 of the Peace Treaty contained a stipulation that the USSR could establish a consulate in Petsamo. The USSR demanded, however, that this consulate could function in a vast district comprising "the town of Petsamo, the entire province of Lapland including the towns Petsamo, Oulu, Tornio, Kemi, Rovaniemi, Kemijarvi and the harbor of Liinahamari." Finland did agree that the district of the consulate should include, in addition to the actual Petsamo area, the entire Province of Lapland.

This willingness of the Finnish authorities to extend the consulate's sphere of action beyond the limits stipulated in the Peace Treaty was abused by the USSR, and attempts were even made to interpret the Petsamo area as including the entire province of Lapland (cf. Documents 58-59). This led to several controversies in connection with the arrangements for the right of travel of members of the consulate staff. The USSR also based on this concession a proposal for establishing a consulate at Rovaniemi, subordinated to the Petsamo consulate. In addition to a consulate, a branch of the commercial section of the Soviet Legation was established in Petsamo. In several instances, members of the Russian consulate in Petsamo were shown to have engaged in espionage; in not a few cases, they were caught attempting to travel to parts of the country where travel is forbidden.

5. *Soviet Disregard of Restrictions on Travel*

Proposals were made by the Soviet Legation, in the autumn of 1940, that more extensive privileges be granted to diplomatic and consular representatives of the USSR in Finland than those permitted by the travel regulations then in force (Document 32). These demands were supported by general references to the Peace Treaty (Document 39). In a Soviet Legation memorandum of November 1940, a demand was presented, in a form that must be regarded as violating ordinary diplomatic usage, for unlimited freedom of movement for officials of the Legation and the consular and commercial representatives in Petsamo (Document 45).

After the USSR had established a consulate in the Aaland Islands, local travel regulations were relaxed for the benefit of the consulate staff, in order to enable its members to travel freely from one police district to another. To facilitate communication with Helsinki certain officials were granted travel permits for prohibited areas valid for three-month periods; similar concessions were granted to certain members of the staff of the Petsamo consulate. The Soviet officials did not even bother to accept these permits. Instead, the Soviet Legation persistently demanded permits for all of its officers and that freedom of travel should be unlimited. It was even demanded that Soviet representatives should be entitled to use submarines as means of transport (Document 45).

Special travel rights were granted to the extent which Finnish authorities regarded as not imperiling the whole system of travel regulations. As the Soviet Legation was promised that individual applications for travel permits would be handled in a spirit of good will and speedily (Document 47), arrangements had in fact been made which should have satisfied all travel needs necessary for legitimate official business. In Soviet quarters, however, the concessions made were regarded as unsatisfactory, and the demand was renewed for unlimited freedom of movement (Document 52). The fact that the representatives of other Powers in Finland enjoyed similar treatment in regard to freedom of movement, and that they had offered no objections to the system in force, was disregarded by the Soviet Legation.

While the question of special travel privileges was to the fore, members of the Legation and consular staffs repeatedly made themselves guilty of willful and gross breaches of the regulations in force, which applied to them as well as to others (Document 48). When Finnish authorities, in the performance of their duties, prevented attempts to enter prohibited areas, they were accused of provocative behavior, etc.; no effort was made to understand the existing system of travel regulations (Documents 39 and 59). The Soviet envoy in Helsinki, M. Zotov, devoted hours to conversations in which, *inter alia,* he defended a subordinate who had been caught traveling under an assumed name and, therefore, had been refused a travel permit.

The persistence with which this question of right to travel was kept in dispute and magnified beyond all reason, together with the specious arguments advanced (Document 52), clearly revealed the absence of any sincere desire in Soviet circles to reach a friendly settlement. It disclosed, rather, a desire to find new opportunities for trouble-making (Document 62).

6. *The Attempt to Deprive Finland of Power from the Vallinkoski Rapids*

In May 1940, the USSR notified Finland that it intended to complete the building of the Enso power plant in accordance with Finnish plans drawn up before the war. The desire was expressed that the rights of both parties should be defined by agreement and USSR and Finnish interests in this matter clarified. Finland acted favorably on the proposal. In the course of negotiations held at Moscow in the summer of 1940, Finland handed over to the USSR the plans for the power plant and delivery contracts which were a part of the plans, as requested by the USSR. During the negotiations Finland proposed, as a practical solution, that the USSR, in return for the right to utilize the water power of the Vallinkoski Rapids,[1] should undertake to supply Finland annually with electric power, free of charge, amounting to 45 per cent of the capacity of the new Enso power plant, or an average of 300 million kwh. per year (of the combined fall of the two rapids, 72 per cent is on the Finnish side of the frontier, and 28 per cent on the Soviet side).

After the negotiations had been concluded, the USSR presented to Finland, in August 1940, a draft proposal (Document 24) in which, wholly disregarding the practical considerations advanced by Finland during the negotiations, and with no attempt at any reasonable justification, the USSR without further ado adopted, as the basis of an agreement, the idea that Russia would get the water power of the Vallinkoski Rapids free of charge. In addition to this Finland was to undertake the regulation of the water level—the extent of this work was not defined—"as proposed by the USSR." Finland's factual counterproposal (Document 36) embodied, in the form of an agreement, the principles advanced by Finland during the summer negotiations. Attention was drawn, *inter alia,* to Finland's undisputed property rights in the Vallinkoski Rapids. Finland was prepared to surrender her right to exploit the rapids only against compensation, which could most suitably be arranged in the form of compensation in kind, i. e., the supply of current. The Finnish Envoy to Moscow, Dr. Paasikivi, presented this counterproposal on November 1, 1940, to M. Molotov, who, because of the Petsamo nickel problem mentioned below, was enraged to find Finland adhering to her rights in the counterproposal (Document 41).

The USSR made no answer until May 13, 1941 (Document 72), when it stated that the USSR clung to its former stand. This stand ignored all Finnish rights. The USSR contended that its draft proposal of the preceding August had "been drafted in full conformity with Article 2 of the Peace Treaty concluded between the USSR and Finland March 12, 1940, Article 6 of the Protocol appended to the said Treaty, and existing international practice." The USSR further declared that under the Peace Treaty it had an undisputed right to complete the building of the Enso power plant in accordance with the original plans and to raise the level of the Vuoksi River as provided in the pre-war Finnish project.

The USSR also refused to pay to the Enso-Gutzeit Company the compensation asked by Finland for the plans, etc., declaring that the Peace Treaty made no provision for compensation for property transferred to the USSR, and that the USSR had assumed no liability for the obligations of individuals or corporations in respect to property ceded to the USSR. This belated Russian attempt to find in the Peace Treaty a basis for its arbitrary demands reveals an exceptional cynicism in the choice of its methods.

---

[1] *Vallinkoski.* Rapids in the River Vuoksi above the Enso factories which were left by the Peace Treaty to Finland. A scheme had been drafted for combining the fall with that of the Enso fall in a single power plant.

CHAPTER III

RUSSIAN INTERFERENCE IN THE DOMESTIC
AFFAIRS OF FINLAND

1. DURING the peace negotiations M. Molotov brought up the case of the Red Army officer, Leo Antikainen, then serving sentence for treason, and was promised that the matter would be investigated. Soon after the Peace Treaty went into effect, M. Molotov demanded the release not only of Antikainen, but of another criminal, Adolf Taimi, as well. They were freed by Presidential pardon and went to the USSR. In spite of the express assurances of M. Molotov that Antikainen would not cause Finland any further trouble, he has frequently made public speeches against Finland, the latest occasion being in June 1941. As late as June 17 last, a Russian proposal was received that a certain person undergoing punishment for espionage be released and sent to the USSR.

2. Systematic attempts were made by the USSR to interfere in Finnish domestic affairs by supporting the treasonable activities of the "Society for Peace and Friendship between Finland and the USSR." This support was not confined to semiofficial Russian newspaper articles of a tendentious and distorted kind, defending the society; it was also given through diplomatic channels. M. Molotov brought up the case of this society three times in July and August, 1940, and referred to the "persecution" to which, he alleged, the Finnish authorities, and particularly Minister Tanner, were subjecting the society (Documents 22, 23, and 26). M. Zotov also mentioned to the Prime Minister that the society—popularly known as the SNS—was in popular favor in the USSR. In a speech on foreign affairs on August 1, 1940, M. Molotov said: "It should be understood that unless certain elements in the ruling Finnish circles do not cease their repressive measures against those classes of the Finnish population which endeavor to strengthen good neighborly relations with the USSR, the result may be harmful to the relations between the USSR and Finland." The Soviet envoy, M. Zotov, explained the speech to the Finnish Foreign Minister and declared that the development of Finnish-Russian relations would depend on the treatment accorded to the SNS.

An internal Finnish question of imposing restraints on subversive elements, dangerous to the public order, was in this way turned by the USSR into a foreign political issue. Russia thus gave new incitement to the activities of these elements, which, especially in the early part of August 1940, assumed markedly threatening forms in demonstrations and disorders organized by the members of the society. It was insisted in Soviet quarters, however, that it was the society that represented the Finnish people, and that the Finnish Government (by its measures for maintaining order) was guilty of ruthless oppression. The Soviet Legation displayed a lively interest in the society. Members of the Legation staff openly observed its demonstrations and attended meetings organized by the society. Even the head of the Soviet Legation traveled into the country in order to attend its meetings. It can be regarded as certain that the society owed its existence to Soviet initiative. Later in the autumn of 1940, however, USSR interest in it declined.

3. In different connections the USSR exerted pressure to secure the resignation of M. Tanner from the government. When M. Tanner finally did resign, M. Molotov declared that Tanner had merely withdrawn into the background and was still working in opposition to good relations between the USSR and Finland (Document 22 and 26). In a conversation with Foreign Minister Witting on August 18, 1940, M. Zotov said that M. Molotov was of the opinion that the presence in the government of Ministers von Born and Fagerholm did not facilitate the development of friendly relations between Finland and the USSR.

4. On the Finnish Independence Day, December 6, 1940, M. Molotov made a statement to M. Paasikivi which meant far-reaching interference of a threatening nature in the Finnish presidential election of that month (Document 51).

5. Through various broadcasting stations (Petroskoi, Leningrad, the Estonian and Latvian stations), flagrant and violent propaganda was conducted at various times against Finland. In this propaganda special attention was paid to shortcomings of life in Finland, which were exaggerated and compared with the excellent conditions alleged to prevail in the USSR and Estonia. Violent attacks were also made on members of the Finnish Government and other leading public persons, the President of the Republic not excepted. Particularly flagrant were the accusations leveled at M. Tanner and the demands for his resignation from the government. When Prime Minister Ryti was elected President (December 1940), the event was hailed in the Soviet broadcasts with the phrase, "the place of that oppressor of the people, Kallio, has been taken by another oppressor of the people, Ryti, by a so-called majority vote." A term in constant use was "the Tanner-Mannerheim power clique."

6. Compared with the situation before the war, espionage by Soviet diplomatic and consular representatives showed a considerable increase. The Soviet diplomatic and consular staff in Finland more than doubled in size (about two hundred persons were listed as representatives and officials,[1] excluding families). Some ten Finnish-speaking persons alone were employed at the Soviet Legation and listed as members of the diplomatic corps. They and many others

---

[1] The Helsinki Legation alone had 31 persons belonging to the diplomatic corps and 120 assistants.

not familiar with the Finnish language traveled a great deal, moved boldly in prohibited areas under assumed names, and endeavored to keep everything that happened in the country under observation. Information was procured through personal contacts in which enlisted agents were used and relations were maintained with certain Communist circles. Specially close co-operation was maintained by the Soviet Legation with the leaders of the SNS. By these means extensive information of a political and military character was obtained, the latter relating chiefly to defense fortification works. It was ascertained that persons recruited in Estonia and the USSR for this kind of work were taken charge of by Russian Legation officials on their arrival in Finland. The official duties of the Mariehamn and Petsamo consulates were so insignificant compared with the size of the staffs (38 officials in the former and 24 in the latter),[2] that there could be no mistake about the real purpose of those officers. Both consulates worked energetically to gain friends and helpers for the USSR. The consular officers in the Aaland Islands devoted attention to the possibilities which, they believed, local Aaland separatism offered. In Petsamo and in Helsinki, persons sentenced in Finland for treason and relatives of such individuals were employed by the consulates. Attempts were made to gain the favor of the poorer classes by paying lavishly for services, by gifts of material aid, by a friendly demeanor and by praising the USSR to the skies. A number of specially trained spies were also sent to Finland. Every Finn who fell into the hands of Soviet authorities, from prisoners of war upwards, was subjected to attempts to enlist him in the service of the USSR, to induce him to undertake espionage and to convert him into a revolutionary. It was ascertained that persons sent abroad even for fairly short courses were trained to act also in war conditions.

7. The Peace Treaty was supposed to satisfy all Russian desires. During the peace negotiations assurances were received from Soviet delegates that the USSR would not interfere in the domestic affairs of Finland. Thus M. Molotov personally stated during the negotiations, when the new frontier and its distance from the railways on the Soviet side were being discussed, that Finland could construct all the fortifications she wished, and that the USSR would place no obstacles in the way of defense constructions. Nevertheless, the USSR later expressed dissatisfaction on this point also (Document 26).

8. Paragraphs 4 and 5 of Chapter II also refer to Finnish domestic affairs.

---

[2] At the Mariehamn consulate there were 8 consular and 30 other officials. For the sake of comparison it may be mentioned that the staff of the Swedish consulate there comprises a consul and a typist. At the Petsamo consulate there were 3 consular and 21 other officials. The German and British consulates there each have one consul and the 1-2 officials needed in such localities. The Soviet consulate and commercial section there had no duties connected with trade or transit traffic. After the demilitarization of the Aaland Islands had been concluded, the Mariehamn consulate had no official business worth mentioning.

Chapter IV

RUSSIAN EXTORTION OF SPECIAL RIGHTS AND CONCESSIONS

1. *Transit Traffic to Hanko*

AT THE beginning of July 1940, the USSR presented to Finland (inconspicuously inserted between draft agreements relating to normal railway traffic) a proposal for the right to run Soviet trains on the Finnish railroads from Russia to Hanko and back. The USSR went so far in this enterprise as to include in the preamble to the draft agreement, and also in the introductory sentence of the actual agreement, which was to be signed by Finland as well as Russia, a provision according to which the organization of transit traffic to and from Hanko constituted an obligation under the terms of the Peace Treaty (Document 18). M. Molotov, however, had expressly stated to M. Paasikivi, during the peace negotiations, that the Peace Treaty did not presuppose arrangements for transit traffic (Document 23).

In this matter, too, Finland was forced to act under duress. Endeavors were made, therefore, to formulate an arrangement that involved as many traffic regulations as possible. To reduce the drawbacks attaching to the agreement, restriction of military transportation in particular was attempted. A few alleviations were, indeed, secured: thus the number of trains was strictly limited and fairly small; the USSR was to report the trains in advance; the passengers were not to carry arms; each individual had to carry an identification card; traffic charges were placed on a satisfactory basis; and a definite time table was to be observed. On the other hand, the matter had some unsatisfactory aspects: the traffic was carried on by USSR locomotives and railway cars; only two Finnish railway officials were to accompany each train; the transportation of persons in uniform and war material was not prohibited, etc. Although the USSR ultimately agreed in theory to the provision that passengers would be unarmed and that arms belonging to the military would be transported in separate trains, in practice the control of these provisions, and similarly of those relating to the number of passengers and to identification cards, was rendered extremely difficult and downright impossible, because of the attitude of the USSR. This in spite of the fact that the rules relating to the prohibition to carry arms, and to the manner in which arms were to be transported, were agreed upon in an exchange of notes between M. Paasikivi and M. Molotov, which took place simultaneously with the signing of the agreement (September 6, 1940), and was expressly declared an integral part of the agreement. In theory, therefore, Finland escaped some of the grave and especially dangerous military drawbacks, but in actual fact this was not the case.

As the USSR demanded that the agreement should be kept secret, Finland was forced to put it into effect in a manner which deviated from constitutionally approved procedure.

The actual traffic began on September 25, 1940. Especially during the first months it caused great inconvenience to the Finnish railway authorities. Because of the inferior quality of the USSR rolling stock and the general negligence of the Soviet railway officials, trains reached Finnish territory behind schedule; on their runs in Finland they often fell still farther behind schedule, sometimes by many hours, thereby disrupting Finnish traffic. Moreover, the Soviet authorities tended to act in violation of the agreement, thereby threatening the regulations governing railroad traffic. Finland proceeded, however, to take up the matter with all possible energy, with the result that order was generally restored and traffic discipline improved. Yet, a few railway accidents occurred, for which, though they resulted from defective Soviet rolling stock, the USSR invariably tried to put the blame on Finland. As a result of their poor quality and negligence in their care, the USSR locomotives caused many fires along the railway, in May-June 1941. On one occasion, not less than nine fires were started during a single run. Thanks to the efficient lookout by the Finnish guards accompanying the train, the fires were extinguished before causing much damage.

On June 17, 1941, the Soviet Government issued written, malicious and false accusations charging that Finland was not satisfactorily fulfilling the provisions of the agreement. The Finnish representative who was to attend the meeting to discuss these allegations, was not given a visa.

2. *Exposure of the Aaland Islands to Attack*

At the negotiations carried on between Finland and the USSR (Sweden acting as mediator) prior to the conclusion of the Peace Treaty, the USSR declared that just as it was natural for the USSR to hold Hanko for the defense of the entrance to the Gulf of Finland, so it was natural for Sweden to be interested in the defense of the inlet to the Gulf of Bothnia; therefore, the USSR had no objection to the fortification of the Aaland Islands. The Peace Treaty contained no stipulations whatever relating to the Aaland Islands.

Nevertheless, on June 27, 1940, the USSR brought up the question of the Aaland Islands and demanded either their demilitarization or else their fortification jointly with the USSR, and further that the USSR must obtain control over the execution of these measures. This demand (like that relating to the

Petsamo nickel mines) was presented just before the signing of the trade treaty between Finland and the USSR. Although Article 8 of the Peace Treaty provided for the conclusion of a trade treaty without the imposition of any special conditions, the USSR adopted the standpoint that the conclusion of a trade treaty was a special act of good will toward Finland, in return for which Finland would have to consent to certain arrangements not connected with matters covered by the treaty.

To M. Paasikivi's remark that this attitude of the USSR regarding the Aaland Islands differed altogether from its attitude in the autumn of 1939 (Finland may fortify if she does so alone), M. Molotov answered that the USSR had altered its views since the war in this matter as well as in others. He added cynically that he had not wished to take up the subject during the peace negotiations in order to avoid possible new difficulties (Document 16).

The demand for the demilitarization of the Aaland Islands was thus brought forth in a manner that made it impossible for Finland to oppose it without imperiling her relations with the USSR. Yet the question involved an extremely serious Finnish concession which moreover meant an essential change in the existing status of the Aaland Islands. For the new proposal meant that Finland's possibilities of defending the Aaland Islands, as presupposed even by the agreement of 1921, would be reduced almost to zero. In actual fact this meant that the USSR would take advantage of the first favorable opportunity to seize the islands.

On July 3, the USSR was informed that the removal of Finnish troops and armament from the islands was begun. M. Molotov took up on this occasion the question of control, and for that purpose asked Finland's consent to the establishment of a Russian consulate in the Aaland Islands.

After this had been agreed to, the USSR raised the question of a periodic future control, for which purpose Soviet military authorities would visit the islands from time to time. This extremely grave matter for Finland was subsequently allowed to lapse, however.

On July 24, the USSR presented its first draft proposal. It contained no mention of the international agreement of 1921. The Finnish counterproposal, on the other hand, referred specifically to the agreement of 1921 and declared that Finland's rights and obligations under that agreement would not be altered by the new agreement. Attempts were made to secure a settlement which would leave the gun emplacements and unarmed defense works intact for the period of the present Great War, after which Finland and the USSR would jointly agree as to their fate. The USSR would not consent to this. As regards the 1921 agreement, M. Molotov was of the opinion that the article referring to it was unnecessary as, according to him, the old agreement would lapse upon the coming into force of the new agreement (subsequently he altered his standpoint; Document 31).

On September 4, the USSR presented a new draft proposal. It contained among other things the obligation to consult Russia. Finland was to consult with the USSR in the event that she would have to carry out measures envisaged under the 1921 agreement. This clause, the meaning and scope of which had not been specifically defined, was especially serious from the Finnish point of view. It also spelled a material change of the 1921 agreement. Finland could not see her way to agree to this, and indeed she could hardly have done so without the consent of the signatories to the 1921 agreement.

On September 27, Finland presented her counterproposal to the Russian proposal of September 4. It omitted the clause relating to consultations. In its place was put another providing for the obligation to notify the USSR, thus placing the USSR in the same position as the actual signatory powers of 1921. M. Molotov, however, insisted on the consultation clause. He declared that the USSR would not object to having Sweden placed in the same position as the USSR, but other powers should have nothing to do with the Aaland Islands.

On September 30, M. Molotov replied to the Finnish proposal. He said that the USSR could not consent to the dispatch of notes all over Europe (by which he meant the proposal, to be sent to all the signatory powers of 1921, that the USSR be placed in a position similar to the other signatories). He added mockingly that perhaps France, for instance, might not give her consent. Nevertheless, M. Molotov abandoned the demand for consultations but presented a demand, couched in the terms of an ultimatum, that an agreement would have to be concluded within a week (Document 31).

Even in such a purely formal matter as the going into effect of the agreement, the attitude of the USSR was one of contempt for Finnish legal order. When M. Molotov, who had demanded that the agreement should become effective as soon as it had been signed, was informed that under Finnish law it must first be ratified by Parliament, he remarked arrogantly that if the Peace Treaty could become valid without the assistance of Parliament, this "less important matter" could be similarly arranged.

Already before the agreement went into effect the destruction of fixed military defenses on the Aaland Islands had been begun. Notification that troops and arms had been removed was given as early as August 3. The Soviet consulate was given opportunity to follow the work of demilitarization. The consulate did so and fully utilized its large staff for the purpose. The consulate officials generally behaved in a petty manner and were troublesome in demanding that the inspections provided for in Article 3 be performed twice. As they gradually raised their trifling objections, the demolition of the fortifications was not completed to their satisfaction until February 1941. Consul Orlenko demanded the destruction of the Coast Guard barracks (a large part was actually destroyed), the limitation to a minimum of Coast Guard and Pilot personnel, and de facto the disarmament of the Coast Guard vessels regardless of the fact that the Guard had maintained boats of the same type there prior to 1939. The latter demands were rejected.

Since the new agreement became valid (Document 34), the significance of the 1921 agreement has been rather vague. M. Molotov, as shown above, minimized its importance and remarked to M. Paasikivi that it was immaterial to him how Finland interpreted it (Document 31). Similarly the Mariehamn consulate, in presenting the USSR demands, revealed its indifference to the 1921 agreement. For her part, Finland has consistently observed its provisions.

Attempts were at first made to limit the size of the consulate staff by agreement. M. Molotov, however, rejected the idea and said that if there was insufficient work for the consulate the staff would be reduced (Document 29). Nevertheless, after demilitarization had been completed and the duties of the consulate could be regarded as substantially reduced, the USSR abstained from reducing the staff. When Foreign Minister Witting, in the course of a conversation with M. Zotov after the demilitarization had been concluded, drew attention to this matter and inquired whether the staff could not now be reduced, M. Zotov replied that a reduction was impossible because the great number of islands in the group required an enormous amount of work.

3. *Attempts to Gain Control of the Petsamo Nickel Mines*

In the Peace Treaty the USSR "left" Petsamo to Finland. Barely three months later, however, the USSR began to demand this area for itself. Although the demand was concealed under the cloak of economic interests, its true nature stood clearly revealed.

On June 23, M. Molotov intimated that the USSR was interested in the Petsamo Nickel Mines, located not far from Soviet territory, and inquired whether Finland would not give the USSR the mining concession, or agree to the establishment of a joint Finnish-Russian company, or arrange the matter in some other way (Document 14).

Under an agreement concluded in 1934 between the Finnish state and the British-Canadian Mond Nickel Company (a subsidiary of the American-British-owned International Nickel Company), the mining concession belonged to this company. Finland could not, therefore, unilaterally invalidate the concession. As a solution, it was therefore proposed that the USSR buy a part of the output of the mines.

The USSR would not agree to this proposal, although it meant satisfying its economic interests. M. Molotov adopted a more inflexible attitude. He replied, on June 27, that the USSR was interested not only in the ore, but in the territory in which the mines were situated, and in getting rid of the British holders of the concession. To a reference to their legal rights, M. Molotov answered that the Nickel Company would not raise difficulties if Finland wished to withdraw the concession, and that the matter could be arranged in four weeks (Document 15).

In Finland it was considered obvious from the start that the consent of the holders of the concession was essential for any alteration in the right to exploit the mines. The USSR was informed, on July 3, that Finland had taken steps for arranging the matter and was negotiating with the holders of the concession.

Contrary to M. Molotov's assertion, the owners of the concession proved unwilling to surrender their rights.

In July, the USSR reported that it had been in communication with Germany, and that the two Powers had agreed to divide the nickel output; Germany would take 60 per cent and the USSR 40 per cent of the production (Document 19). This was regarded in Finland as a sign that the USSR had abandoned its earlier standpoint, and would be satisfied by guarantees that it could obtain nickel. This view was supported by the fact that Germany, having disclosed an interest in the concession question earlier than Russia, had informed Finland that it had abandoned the idea and would be satisfied with a part of the output of nickel.

The USSR did not return to the subject until late in August, when M. Molotov unexpectedly asked for an answer and stressed the interest of the USSR in the mining concession.

On September 13, M. Paasikivi delivered Finland's reply. It stated that negotiations with the Mond people were not proceeding smoothly. M. Molotov thereupon replied that he regarded the matter as extremely important, the granting of the concession to strangers as contrary to the interests of the USSR, and in conflict with the Peace Treaties of Tartu and Moscow, the USSR having been granted free transit precisely through the nickel area. He stated again that the USSR was interested in the area as such (Document 27). On September 30, M. Molotov again urged haste in the matter, remarking that it had been pending for some months. On October 9, M. Molotov made a new demand for an answer, and declared that the British Ambassador in Moscow, Cripps, had been notified already in July that Great Britain would not object to an agreement between Finland and the USSR regarding the exploitation of the mines.

In pressing Finland for an affirmative answer, the USSR hinted at its readiness to resort to "other measures" and displayed an almost complete indifference to the legal considerations which were a determining factor in Finland's attitude. On October 30, the Assistant Commissar for Foreign Affairs, Vyshinski, complained about the delay and answered M. Paasikivi's remark that Finland could not take over the concession without the consent of the owners by saying that, if this were Finland's final reply, the USSR would be compelled to proceed to necessary measures. M. Vyshinski poked fun at Finland's attitude, asking whether Finland was a British colony, and requested an answer within two or three days (Document 37). M. Paasikivi reported that he had formed the idea that M. Molotov seemed to accept Finland's standpoint, according to which the consent of the Nickel Company was essential, whereas M. Vyshinski paid no attention to this view.

Finland had no wish, in view of the menacing language used by the USSR, to obstruct a transfer of this concession. As Finland, however, had not received the consent of the holders of the concession, which was an essential condition for the transfer, she was willing to give the USSR an opportunity to secure this consent. On October 31, Prime Minister Risto Ryti presented an answer to that effect to M. Zotov (Document 38). M. Paasikivi received instructions to present the same suggestion at the Kremlin. But before the telegram instructing him to do so arrived, he had a conversation with M. Molotov on November 1. The latter had protested in sharp terms against the delay and hinted that the USSR would proceed to action if the matter was not speedily settled (Document 41).

On November 5, M. Paasikivi laid before M. Vyshinski the suggestion Prime Minister Ryti had made to M. Zotov. M. Vyshinski was of the opinion that Finland could unilaterally invalidate the concession, alleging that the matter was clear as far as Great Britain was concerned. Finland, as the owner of the mines, was therefore free to do with them as she wished. In regard to Germany, too, which had shown an interest in the mining concession before Russia, and had later concluded an agreement concerning the output of nickel, M. Vyshinski alleged that the matter was in order (Document 42).

Through the Finnish Minister in London, M. Gripenberg, it was learned on November 7 that the account given by the USSR of Great Britain's attitude was erroneous and that, in the opinion of the Foreign Office, Finland could inform the USSR that the matter would not be clear as far as Great Britain was concerned until the USSR had agreed to export no nickel to Germany (Document 43).

The USSR had thus not secured the consent of the owners of the mining concession. Despite this, the USSR still held that a transfer of the concession could be made, and demanded that Finland should take away the concession from its owners; the question of principle and legality was brushed aside as unimportant. On November 12, M. Vyshinski told M. Paasikivi that the USSR would no longer negotiate with either Great Britain or Germany, and that it was in Finland's power to settle the matter if she only desired to do so. Finland could simply inform Great Britain that the concession would be canceled to clear the way for other arrangements. If Finland failed to proceed in this way, the USSR would interpret failure to act as a refusal. To M. Paasikivi's remark about the legal side of the question, M. Vyshinski replied that if no suitable law existed, one could be enacted. He pointed out, in private conversation, that the USSR could have retained Petsamo on the conclusion of both the Tartu Treaty of 1920 and the Moscow Peace Treaty of 1940 (Document 44).

On November 15, haste was urged once more, this time through M. Zotov, who again argued that neither Great Britain nor Germany had any objection to a transfer of the concession.

On November 19, M. Molotov told M. Paasikivi that he had conversed with Berlin on the subject of Petsamo nickel, and informed him that Germany abandoned its claim to the concession and offered no objection to its transfer to the USSR. M. Molotov corrected M. Paasikivi's view that he, Molotov, had been of the opinion that the assent of Great Britain and the Nickel Company was essential. Finland would have to arrange the matter in one way or another (Document 46).

It soon became apparent that Germany, contrary to the statements by M. Zotov and M. Molotov, was not prepared, any more than Great Britain had been, for an unconditional transfer of the concession. Germany informed Finland and the USSR on November 25 of its conditions, the gist of which was that if a new company were formed, it would have to assume responsibility for the agreements concluded between the existing company and the German I. G. Farbenindustrie.

On November 26, M. Paasikivi was instructed to propose to the Commissariat for Foreign Affairs that, in order to gain time while a definite answer was being awaited from Great Britain (which Finland was still endeavoring to procure), Finland and the USSR should draft an agreement for a Finnish-Russian nickel company and for the transfer to it of the mining concession in its entirety. On December 3, he proposed to M. Molotov that a mixed committee should be appointed for this purpose. M. Molotov agreed.

The directives given to the Finnish members of the mixed committee were that they should try to obtain an arrangement under which a Finnish-Russian company would be founded, but the existing setup would be preserved as far as possible, the present nickel company to be in charge of mining operations and the new Finnish-Russian company of sales.

The first negotiations in the mixed committee were held in Moscow on December 19-23, 1940. The company proposed by Finland, which would have assured the speediest solution of the question, failed to gain support. The USSR insisted on the following: a company which would operate the mines as well as the concession; a majority of the stock of the company; one-half of the Board of Directors whose chairmanship would alternately be Finnish and Russian; the posts of Managing Director and Mines Manager; and (a supplementary demand made in January) that 20 per cent of the technical staff should be Russian. As unanimity could not be reached, the Finnish delegates returned to Helsinki to confer with their government.

Early in January 1941, the USSR pressed for the speedy return of the Finnish delegates. On January 14, M. Vyshinski told M. Paasikivi that the USSR demanded an answer, for its patience was now exhausted. If a settlement could not be reached by friendly negotiation, the USSR would find other means to settle the matter. He declared that the Finnish Government was holding up the matter on all kinds of pretexts (Document 60). On January 21, M. Vyshinski again insisted on a speedy answer. M. Paasikivi explained that, in spite of every effort, Finland had not been able to come to an arrangement with Great Britain, that the important question of compensating the owners of the concession was still open, and that Finland had wished to await information of the negotiations which a special delegate, Dr. H. Ramsay, was conducting in London. M. Vyshinski called these Finnish explanations mere excuses to which he did not want to listen, and demanded a final answer from Finland by January 23. If the reply were not forthcoming by that date, he would inform his government of Finland's refusal. M. Vyshinski repeated his statement that the USSR had "given" Petsamo to Finland (Document 61).

On January 23, M. Paasikivi informed M. Vyshinski that Finland was prepared to negotiate. The negotiations were resumed in Moscow on January 29. It became apparent that the Soviet had no desire to draw any nearer to the Finnish proposal, and that the earlier demands were still stubbornly maintained. As a breakdown of the negotiations was hardly to be avoided in the circumstances (with all the dangerous consequences which Russia had repeatedly hinted at) Finland was once again forced, under duress, to go a long step farther in her concessions.

Finland presented a draft agreement in which she promised to take possession of the mines and to surrender their administration and exploitation to a Finnish-Russian company. Finland thus retreated from her earlier stand. Finland, however, was to hold a controlling interest and a majority of the board of directors, and the managing director and mining staff were to be Finnish.

Despite this readiness of Finland to reach a settlement by making far-reaching concessions, the USSR showed no desire whatever to achieve a settlement by ordinary means of negotiation. It would not accept a Finnish management ("unreasonable and unacceptable even as a basis for discussion"), but adhered to its demands for "equality" on the board and for the managing directorship (Documents 63-65). As the work of the mixed committee failed to proceed wholly to the liking of the USSR, the USSR simultaneously brought pressure to bear on Finland and presented threats through diplomatic channels.

On February 12, M. Vyshinski had a talk with M. Paasikivi. He declared that the USSR had no ulterior motives, but was pursuing merely economic objectives. Equality in the leadership of the company was demanded (argument: the USSR is a Great Power and Finland a small nation, ergo the prestige of the USSR called for equality—Document 65). During the same conversation, M. Vyshinski remarked that Finland and the USSR were involved in a trade war (Document 66).

The mixed committee held its last meeting on February 15, at which Finland made certain concessions but adhered to her demand that the posts of Managing Director and Chairman of the Board, the local management and the appointment also of minor officers, with a couple of exceptions, would be reserved to Finland. The date of the next meeting of the mixed committee was fixed for February 17, but at the last minute the meeting was canceled. The reason given was that the chairman of the Soviet delegation had been taken ill. No invitation, however, to a new meeting was later received, and subsequent negotiations were conducted solely through diplomatic channels.

On February 18, M. Vyshinski interpreted the Finnish standpoint to M. Paasikivi as negative. He declared that there was no reason to continue with the work of the mixed committee. The USSR demands were categorical. Nothing could be done. The matter, with all its consequences, would now have to take its own course (Document 67).

In form as well as substance, the negotiations were thus broken off by the USSR, which refused to reduce even slightly its excessive demands. Finland, for her part, instructed the Finnish delegates to remain in Moscow for the eventuality that contact could be re-established. The USSR, however, did not avail itself of the opportunity to resume negotiations but compelled the Finnish delegates, by refusing them permits to stay or curtailing permits already given, to return to Finland. The chairman of the Finnish delegation, M. von Fieandt, whose permit was valid for a longer stay, remained in Moscow until March 8.

On March 4, M. Molotov expressed his regret to M. Paasikivi over the failure of the negotiations. M. Molotov repeated once again his assertion about the good will that the USSR had shown in "surrendering" Petsamo to Finland.[1] He demanded for the USSR the post of managing director and said that the intentions of the USSR were solely of an economic character (Document 68).

After this conversation on March 4, there was no further contact (except for conversations on the occasions of the first visits by the new Soviet Minister, M. Orlov, in Helsinki) with the USSR on the subject of the nickel mines until May 5, when Foreign Minister Witting, in the course of a general conversation with M. Orlov, suggested that the USSR might consider the abandonment of its demand for a mixed company and that the matter might be arranged as a purely economic question without interfering with the mining concession, adding that Finland would, if requested, adhere to her earlier concessions (Document 69). Finland gave her final answer on May 10, in which she maintained her former attitude, *inter alia,* in regard to the post of Managing Director, and again stressed her desire to continue negotiations (Documents 70-71). M. Vyshinski promised to lay the answer before his government, but stated that he could say beforehand that the answer would not satisfy the

---

[1] This assertion, frequently advanced, is a deliberate distortion of facts. The Petsamo area was promised to Finland already in an agreement of 1864 by the Russian Government in return for the cession by Finland to Russia of the Siestarjoki rifle factory area on the Karelian Isthmus. In the Tartu peace treaty, Lenin fulfilled this obligation. In the Moscow peace treaty the provision relating to Petsamo is as binding on the USSR as any other of the peace terms.

Soviet Government. After that date, the USSR did not again refer to this question of the nickel mines.

It was illustrative of the Soviet attitude in the nickel question that while Finland was being assured that the question was merely economic in character, the USSR was simultaneously underlining to one of the Great Powers the military-political nature of the problem.

CHAPTER V

TRADE BETWEEN FINLAND AND THE USSR, 1940-1941

ON JUNE 28, 1940, a trade treaty was concluded in Moscow between Finland and the USSR. In it the commercial quotas of both parties were fixed for the period July 1, 1940–June 30, 1941. A clearing agreement was simultaneously concluded. It assumed that payments made by one party to the other would be kept balanced.

Quota goods were thereafter exported on both sides, until the USSR stopped all exports to Finland at the beginning of January 1941. The alleged reason was that Finnish exports to the USSR had been too small compared with USSR exports to Finland, and that consequently the balance in the exchange of goods had been disturbed. In this manner the USSR, in violation of the trade treaty, opened a trade war on Finland.

This Soviet action clearly ran counter to the clearing agreement, which expressly stipulated that a disturbance in the *balance of payments* would justify the stoppage of exports. The balance of payments had in fact developed according to the terms of the clearing agreement; it would have been impossible for the USSR to make any complaint on that score. The major part of the aggregate value of the Finnish goods quotas was represented by tugs and lighters of which about 45 per cent were scheduled for delivery during the first year of the treaty and the rest during the second year. The time required to draft the contracts for these vessels, the progress of actual construction and the advance and part payments connected with their building are essential factors in judging the rate of Finnish deliveries. The contracts for the vessels were concluded with the Soviet import organization at the end of the first quarter of the first treaty-year; periods of delivery were correspondingly postponed. The delay in drafting the final contracts did not depend on the Finnish Government or the Finnish shipyards. On the contrary, both did their utmost to secure fulfillment of the contracts within the stipulated time, despite difficulties in obtaining raw materials.

An examination of the clearing account shows that the statement by the USSR that Finland had not fulfilled her obligations was altogether unfounded. Article 7 of the clearing agreement stipulated that the aggregate payments on both sides should balance. On June 18, the clearing account showed that

Finland had a claim of $310,638 on the USSR.[1] The clearing situation, therefore, did not justify a stoppage of USSR exports; on the contrary, it called for increased exports by the USSR.

The USSR export of quota goods to Finland having been at a standstill during the current year, the USSR failed, during the first treaty-year (ending on June 30, 1941), to deliver the following quotas:

    35,000 tons of grain
    18,800 tons of apatite
     5,000 tons of gasoil
    14,000 tons of petroleum
     8,000 tons of gasoline
       300 tons of lubricating oil
        30 tons of paraffin
     1,000 tons of manganese ore
     1,250 tons of cotton
     3,400 tons of oilcakes

It may be added that the USSR did not deliver to Finland a single drop of the gasoline quota. A certain quantity of gasoline was, it is true, purchased from the USSR, but this quantity was not delivered on a treaty basis under the clearing agreement, as it had to be paid for in cash. Of the grain quota agreed upon, the USSR delivered only one half, including the last consignment of 20,000 tons which Moscow has so loudly advertised.

---

[1] Finnish liabilities on Finnish-Estonian and Finnish-Latvian accounts, totaling $877,800, had been transferred to the clearing account. In spite of this, the account showed the balance mentioned in Finland's favor.

Chapter VI

VIOLATIONS OF FINNISH TERRITORY BY THE USSR

A. *Aircraft*

1940: March .... 1 case
April .... none
May .... 1 case
June .... 5 cases
July .... 6 cases
August .... 7 cases
September .... 2 cases
October .... 5 cases
November .... none
December .... none

1941: January .... 8 cases
February .... 5 cases
March .... 19 cases
April .... 5 cases
May .... 13 cases
June .... 8 cases (up to June 21)

Total: 85 cases

Notification of these violations of Finnish territory was made to the Soviet authorities in each instance without delay by the respective frontier commissioners. The Soviet authorities replied only in four cases, viz., in writing, regarding the violations on September 24, 1940, and March 28, 1941; and orally regarding the violations on April 2 and May 22, 1941, admitting that Soviet aircraft, owing to navigational errors, had crossed the frontier by mistake.

B. *Other Violations*

1940: March .... 5 frontier violations
April .... 24 " "
May .... 17 " "
June .... 10 " "
July .... 12 " "
August .... 7 " "

1940: September .... 5 frontier violations
       October 4   "   "
       November 5   "   "
       December 5   "   "

1941: January .... 5 frontier violations
       February .... none
       March .... 2 frontier violations
       April 1   "   "
       May 1   "   "
       June 6   "   "   (up to June 26)

Total: 109 frontier violations

The second tabulation does not include violations of Finnish territory by aircraft. Primarily, it comprises movements by vessels of the USSR Navy into Finnish territorial waters, the crossing of the frontier by patrols and scouts, shots fired across the frontier, etc. Each of the violations included in the statistics was immediately reported to the Soviet authorities by the respective frontier commissioners. The Soviet authorities replied but rarely.

C. *The Shooting Down of the Airplane "Kaleva"*

According to undisputed facts in the possession of the Finnish Government, Russian aircraft shot down, on June 14, 1940, the passenger airplane *Kaleva* of Aerohansa model, flying on the route between Helsinki and Tallinn.

The course of events was as follows: On June 14, at 2 P.M., two Russian SB-2 aircraft attacked the *Kaleva* and shot her down into the sea off the Ker lighthouse. Afterward the aircraft made off in an easterly direction. The Russian submarine Q-301 arrived on the scene of the incident and salvaged the mail, including diplomatic mail, weighing about 230 lbs. in all. The mail was transferred on June 15 to a certain vessel which took it to Kronstadt (Document 13). The passengers on board the *Kaleva,* all of whom were killed, included two Germans, two Frenchmen, one American, one Swede, and one Estonian.

Chapter VII

POLICY OF PRESSURE ENDS IN ATTACK

IMMEDIATELY after the outbreak of war between Germany and the USSR on June 22, 1941, the armed forces of the USSR began to carry out attacks on Finnish territory, dropping bombs on and machine-gunning purely Finnish objectives. Already the first air attacks were of a flagrant character, being aimed at the Finnish Fort Alskaer and at two Finnish war vessels engaged in the execution of the measures of security provided for in the Agreement of 1921 relating to the nonfortification and neutralization of the Aaland Islands. On the same day fire was opened from Soviet territory on Finnish frontier guards in the vicinity of Immola, and from Pummanki several dozen shells were fired at a Finnish vessel.

With reference to the first violations of Finnish territory, Foreign Minister Witting presented a protest on June 22 to M. Orlov and requested an explanation. M. Orlov promised to report to his government but no explanation was ever received (Document 73).

On the evening of June 23, the Finnish Minister in Moscow, M. Hynninen, was invited to call on M. Molotov. The latter demanded information from M. Hynninen regarding the attitude of the Finnish Government in the situation created by the war between Germany and the USSR and declared, as he had done in his speech on the preceding day, that attacks had been launched on the USSR from Finnish territory. Less than twenty-four hours later, before the Finnish Government had had time to answer M. Hynninen's telegram reporting the conversation (it arrived in the night of June 24-25), the USSR launched, on June 25, an all-out attack on Finland and thus opened hostilities.

If it might have been possible to regard the previous attacks as mere incidents, the general offensive begun on June 25 revealed beyond all doubt that the policy of the USSR toward Finland was war. Prior to this general Russian offensive no forces of any kind, either Finnish or German, had attacked USSR territory from Finland.

After the USSR had embarked on organized warfare against Finland, Prime Minister Rangell, in view of the situation thus created, made a statement, on June 25 at 5 P.M. to the Finnish Parliament on behalf of the government.

On June 26, the following communiqué was issued: "At the meeting of the

Parliament yesterday, Prime Minister Rangell made a statement of the present situation and of the circumstances which had led up to it. The Prime Minister took note of the fact that since yesterday Finland has been the object of an attack by the USSR which had opened hostilities against Finland. In consequence, Finland has proceeded to defend herself with all the military means at her disposal. After hearing the Prime Minister's statement, the Parliament unanimously passed a vote of confidence in the Government."

On the same day, President Risto Ryti broadcast a speech to the Finnish nation, in the closing part of which he said among other things:

"The trend of the Soviet Union's activities toward us is clear from all that I have submitted to you. The independence of Finland was to be destroyed, either with the aid of domestic upheavals and difficulties, or else by the forcible conquest of the country. When the path of domestic revolution was seen to be closed because of our nation's great love of liberty, and of our internal unity, the Soviet Union decided to embark on the path of violence.

"With this in mind M. Molotov demanded of Germany, in the course of the Berlin negotiations of November 12-13, 1940 (only seven months after the Peace of Moscow!) a free hand to strike a final blow at Finland and to liquidate us. . . .

"Ever since the outbreak of the present Great War, the intentions and attitude of the Soviet Union in this war have been clearly evident. The Soviet Union watched with satisfaction the outbreak of the conflict, and aimed all the time at extending and prolonging it as much as possible in order that the European nations and, if possible, nations outside of Europe as well, might thereby be materially and morally weakened and their powers of resistance to Bolshevist agitation reduced, so that they would fall an easy prey to Soviet imperialism when, in the opinion of the Soviet Union, the appropriate moment for its armed intervention in the war had come.

"The Soviet Union has ruthlessly exploited various situations with the result that our country, too, while the war between the Great Powers raged on other fronts, had to meet, unaided, the immense superiority of the Soviet Union. We do not hate the long-suffering and oppressed peoples of the Soviet Union, but after all that has happened we can hardly be expected to go into mourning because M. Molotov, and with him the circles responsible for Russia's policy, now have fallen victims to their own policy which has been the policy of scavengers.

"Now that the Soviet Union, as a part of the struggle between Germany and the Soviet Union, has extended hostilities to Finnish territory by attacking this peaceful nation, it is our duty to defend ourselves. We shall do so, determined and united, with all the military and moral resources at our disposal" (Document 74).

TREATY OF PEACE

BETWEEN THE REPUBLIC OF FINLAND AND THE UNION OF SOVIET SOCIALIST REPUBLICS

The Government of the Republic of Finland, of the one part, and

The Presidium of the Supreme Council of the Union of Soviet Socialist Republics, of the other part,

Being desirous of bringing to an end the hostilities which have broken out between the two States and of creating permanent peaceful relations between them,

And being convinced that the creation of definite conditions for their mutual security, including guarantees for the security of the cities of Leningrad and Murmansk and the Murmansk Railway, is in the interests of both Contracting Parties,

Have decided that for this purpose the conclusion of a Peace Treaty is essential and have therefore appointed as their Plenipotentiaries:

The Government of the Republic of Finland:

Risto Ryti, Prime Minister of the Republic of Finland,
Juho Kusti Paasikivi, Minister,
Rudolf Walden, General,
Väinö Voionmaa, Professor.

The Presidium of the Supreme Council of the Union of Soviet Socialist Republics:

Vjatsheslav Mihailovitsh Molotov, President of the Council of Commissars of the USSR and Commissar for Foreign Affairs.
Andrei Aleksandrovitsh Shdanov, Member of the Presidium of the Supreme Council of the USSR.
Aleksander Mihailovitsh Vasilevski, Brigadier;

who, having exchanged their credentials, found in due and proper order, have agreed upon the following provisions:

Article 1

Hostilities between Finland and the USSR shall be immediately concluded according to the procedure defined in the protocol attached to the present Treaty.

Article 2

The frontier between the Republic of Finland and the USSR shall follow a new boundary line which shall incorporate in the territory of the USSR the whole of the Karelian Isthmus, the city of Viipuri and Viipuri Bay with the Islands thereof, the western and northern coastal area of Lake Ladoga with the towns of Käkisalmi and Sortavala and the village of Suojärvi, a number of islands in the Gulf of Finland, the territory east of Märkäjärvi and the village of Kuolajärvi, and parts of the Rybachi and Sredni Peninsulas—in conformity with the map attached to the present Treaty.

The exact delimitation and establishment of the frontier line shall be effected by a mixed committee of representatives of the Contracting Parties, which shall be appointed within ten days of the signing of the present Treaty.

Article 3

Both Contracting Parties undertake to refrain from all acts of aggression directed against each other, and undertake not to conclude any alliance or to become parties to any coalition directed against either of the Contracting Parties.

Article 4

The Republic of Finland agrees to lease to the Soviet Union for thirty years, in consideration of an annual rent of eight million Finnish marks to be paid by the Soviet Union, the cape of Hanko and the surrounding waters within a radius of five nautical miles to the south and east and three nautical miles to the west and north thereof, and a number of islands situated therein, in conformity with the map attached to the present Treaty—for the establishment of a naval base capable of defending the access to the Gulf of Finland against aggressions; and in addition for the defense of the naval base the Soviet Union is granted the right to maintain there at its own expense essential armed land and air forces.

The Government of Finland will withdraw within ten days of the entry into force of the present Treaty the whole of its armed forces from the cape of Hanko, and the cape of Hanko with the islands appertaining thereto will pass into the administration of the USSR in conformity with this Article of the present Treaty.

Article 5

The USSR undertakes to withdraw its military forces from the Petsamo area which the USSR voluntarily ceded to Finland under the terms of the Peace Treaty of 1920.

Finland undertakes, as provided in the Peace Treaty of 1920, not to maintain warships and other armed vessels in the waters along the Arctic coast belonging to it, with the exception of armed vessels of less than one hundred tons, which Finland may maintain there without limit, and a maximum of fifteen war vessels or other armed ships, the tonnage of which may in no case exceed four hundred tons.

Finland undertakes, as provided in the said Treaty, not to maintain submarines and armed aircraft in the waters mentioned.

Finland further undertakes, as provided in the said Treaty, not to construct on this coast any naval harbors, naval bases or naval repair yards which are larger in size than is necessary for the said vessels and their armament.

Article 6

The Soviet Union and its nationals, as provided in the Treaty of 1920, are granted free right of transit through the Petsamo area to and from Norway, and the Soviet Union is granted the right to establish a consulate in the Petsamo area.

Goods transported through the Petsamo area from the Soviet Union to Norway, likewise goods transported through the said area from Norway to the Soviet Union, shall be free of all inspection and control, with the exception of the control necessary for the conduct of transit traffic; nor shall customs duties or transit or other charges be imposed.

Control of the abovementioned transit goods shall be permitted only according to the established practice in such cases in international traffic.

Nationals of the Soviet Union who travel through the Petsamo area to Norway and from Norway back to the Soviet Union, shall be entitled to unhindered passage with passports issued by the appropriate authorities of the Soviet Union.

With due observance of the general provisions in force, unarmed aircraft of the Soviet Union shall be entitled to maintain air traffic between the Soviet Union and Norway through the Petsamo area.

Article 7

The Government of Finland grants to the Soviet Union goods transit rights between the Soviet Union and Sweden, and for the development of this traffic by the shortest railway route the Soviet Union and Finland regard as necessary the construction, each in its own territory, and if possible in the course of the year 1940, of a railway connecting Kandalaksha with Kemijärvi.

Article 8

With the entry into force of the present Treaty, trade relations between the Contracting Parties shall be renewed and for this purpose the Contracting Parties shall proceed to negotiate regarding the conclusion of a Trade Agreement.

Article 9

This Peace Treaty shall enter into force immediately after its signature and shall later be ratified.

The exchange of instruments of ratification shall take place within ten days at Moscow.

The present treaty is drawn up in duplicate in the Finnish, Swedish and Russian languages, in the City of Moscow on March 12, 1940.

Risto Ryti	V. Molotov
J. K. Paasikivi	A. Shdanov
R. Walden	A. Vasilevski
Väinö Voionmaa	

PROTOCOL

attached to the Treaty of Peace concluded between Finland and the Union of Soviet Socialist Republics on March 12, 1940.

The Contracting Parties establish the following procedure for the cessation of hostilities and the transfer of troops behind the frontier fixed by the Treaty of Peace.

1. Both Contracting Parties shall cease hostilities on the 13th day of March, 1940, at twelve o'clock noon Leningrad time.

2. Beginning with the moment agreed upon as the close of the hostilities, a neutral zone one kilometer wide shall be arranged between the advance positions of the troops, for which purpose the troops of that Contracting Party which, with reference to the new frontier, occupies territory belonging to the other Contracting Party, shall be withdrawn a distance of one kilometer on the first day.

3. The transfer of military forces to the other side of the new frontier and the movement of the military forces of the other Contracting Party to that frontier, shall begin at 10 A.M. on March 15, 1940, along the whole of the frontier between the Gulf of Finland and Lieksa, and at 10 A.M. on March 16, north of Lieksa. The transfer shall be effected in marches of not less than 7

kilometers per day, the troops of the other Contracting Party moving forward in such order that an intervening distance of not less than 7 kilometers is maintained between the rearguard of the withdrawing troops and the advance guard of the other Contracting Party moving toward the new frontier.

4. In accordance with Clause 3, the following time limits are fixed for the transfer of troops to the various sections of the frontier:

(*a*) in the sector comprising the upper reaches of the Tuntsajoki River, Kuolajärvi, Takala, the eastern shore of Lake Joukamojärvi, the transfer of the troops of both Contracting Parties shall be completed at 8 P.M. on March 20, 1940;

(*b*) in the Latva sector south of Kuhmoniemi, the transfer of troops shall be completed at 8 P.M. on March 22, 1940;

(*c*) in the sector Lonkavaara, Värtsilä, Matkaselkä railway station, the transfer of the troops of both Contracting Parties shall be completed at 8 P.M on March 26, 1940;

(*d*) in the sector Matkaselkä railway station, Koitsanlahti, the transfer of troops shall be completed at 8 P.M. on March 22, 1940;

(*e*) in the sector Koitsanlahti, Enso railway station, the transfer of troops shall be completed at 8 P.M. on March 25, 1940;

(*f*) in the sector Enso railway station, Paationsaari, the transfer of troops shall be completed at 8 P.M. on March 19, 1940;

5. The evacuation of Red Army troops from the Petsamo area shall be completed by April 10, 1940.

6. The Army Commands of both Contracting Parties undertake, during the transfer of troops to the other side of the frontier, to take necessary measures, in the towns and localities to be ceded to the other Contracting Party, to preserve them from damage and to take necessary measures to preserve towns, localities, defensive and economic establishments (bridges, dams, aerodromes, barracks, depots, railway junctions, industrial establishments, the telegraph system, electric power stations) from damage and destruction.

7. All questions arising out of the cession by one Contracting Party to the other of the areas, localities, towns or other objects mentioned in Clause 6 of the present protocol, shall be decided on the spot by representatives of both Contracting Parties, for which purpose the Army Commands shall appoint special delegates on each of the main routes utilized by both Armies.

8. The exchange of prisoners of war shall be effected with the minimum of delay after the cessation of hostilities in accordance with a special agreement.

March 12, 1940

RISTO RYTI	V. MOLOTOV
J. K. PAASIKIVI	A. SHDANOV
R. WALDEN	A. VASILEVSKI
VÄINÖ VOIONMAA	

DOCUMENTS

Document 1

Extract from Speech Delivered in the Swedish Parliament by the Minister for Foreign Affairs, M. Günther, on March 13, 1940

[*Helsinki Press*, March 14, 1940]

We have learned, in a manner we shall never forget, how closely the fates of the people of the North are bound to each other. This is the reason why these nations must stand ready, more purposefully than ever before, to direct their policy to vital common questions, and to consider objectively, on the basis of our new experiences, the question of strengthening co-operation among the peoples of the North.

Document 2

Discussion of a Defensive Alliance

[*Helsinki Press*, March 15, 1940]

The Government Information Bureau reports: In connection with the conversations with the Swedish and Norwegian Governments arising out of the Finnish war, the possibilities of the establishment of a defensive alliance between Finland, Norway and Sweden, to secure their frontiers and independence, has also been discussed. During the war, this proved to be not feasible. The three governments have agreed, however, that after the conclusion of peace the question will be reconsidered.

Stockholm, March 14, 1940 (Finnish News Agency): As a result of an inquiry by the Finnish Government, the Swedish Government stated that it is prepared to look into the possibilities of bringing a defensive alliance into being.

Oslo, March 14, 1940 (Finnish News Agency): As a result of a telegram received from Helsinki concerning plans for a northern defensive alliance, the Norwegian Telegram Bureau has approached the Minister for Foreign Affairs, M. Koht, who made the following statement:

The Finnish Government inquired, a couple of days ago, of the Norwegian Government whether it would be willing to investigate the possibilities of establishing a defensive alliance between Norway, Sweden and Finland. To this inquiry, the Norwegian Government answered: Yes.

Document 3

[*Helsinki Press*, March 21, 1940]

Moscow, March 20, 1940 (Finnish News Agency): The Soviet News Agency Tass reports: It has been reported in the foreign press that negotiations are proceeding between Finland, Sweden and Norway regarding the conclusion of a so-called defensive alliance, whose business would be the military defense of Finland's frontiers. It is also reported that the Soviet Union would not oppose the establishment of such a "defensive alliance" between Finland, Sweden and Norway.

The Tass Agency is authorized to say that these reports concerning the stand of the USSR do not correspond with the facts, for this kind of an alliance would be directed against the Soviet Union—as is revealed by the strongly anti-Soviet speech made on March 14 in the Norwegian Parliament by the Speaker of the Parliament, Mr. Hambro—and would run altogether counter to the Peace Treaty concluded by the USSR and Finland on March 12, 1940.

Document 4

[*Helsinki Press*, March 21, 1940]

Stockholm, March 20, 1940 (Finnish News Agency): As a result of the statement published by the Tass Agency concerning the contemplated defensive alliance between Sweden, Finland and Norway, the Swedish Minister for Foreign Affairs, M. Günther, stated to the Finnish News Agency that the Russian statement regarding the purpose of the alliance does not correspond to fact but rests on a misconception. That is to say, there is no question whatever of anything but a purely defensive alliance which aims at common action against a possible aggressor.

Document 5

Notes on a Kremlin Conversation Held at 10 p.m. on March 21, 1940

Molotov: For my part, I would like to state the following: Newspapers in the North have recently discussed the question of a defensive alliance between Finland, Sweden and Norway. At the same time, the news was circulated that the Soviet Union would not oppose such an alliance. In an official communication which presumably is known to you, gentlemen, the Tass News Agency has repudiated these contentions regarding the attitude of the USSR toward the contemplated alliance.

According to the newspapers, Finland took the initiative in this alliance matter. What the nature of the alliance would actually be, is clearly revealed by a statement made by the Speaker of the Norwegian Parliament, Mr. Hambro, which contains, among other things, the remark that the new eastern boundary of Finland is only temporary and must be rectified. In other words, the purpose is to get revenge for the Peace Treaty recently concluded. For Finland to participate in such an alliance would mean not only a breach of Article 3 of the treaty, but a violation of the whole treaty because the intention of the alliance is to violate the boundaries by the Peace Treaty. In form, the alliance would possibly be a defensive alliance; actually it would be an instrument of revenge.

We informed the Swedish Government that the conclusion of that kind of alliance with Finland would mean the abandonment of Swedish neutrality, and that if Sweden intends to change its foreign policy toward the USSR, the stand taken by the USSR toward Sweden will be different from what it has been in the past. The Government of Norway has been similarly informed.

Paasikivi: As regards Hambro's statement, we know of it only through newspaper reports and are not responsible for words uttered by him. The notion of revenge is altogether alien to the idea of a defensive alliance, for the reason, if for no other, that Sweden and Norway could never conclude any but a purely defensive alliance. A defensive alliance of this nature would not in any way be directed against the USSR, for one of its purposes would be to secure the present frontiers of Finland, and thus to preserve the status quo. Article 3 of the Peace Treaty does not forbid purely defensive alliances. You may rest assured that neither Sweden nor Norway would conclude any aggressive alliance. All the northern newspapers similarly emphasize that there can be no question of anything but a purely defensive alliance. In our opinion the USSR can have no objection to such a defensive alliance. Finland is neutral, as is Sweden, and we do not interfere in the affairs of other states. Last autumn you and M. Stalin said that Finnish neutrality is in keeping with the interests of the USSR. I have read the Tass repudiation concerning the defensive alliance. Personally I do not know whether Hambro is still the speaker of the Norwegian Storting, or only the Chairman of the Foreign Reations Committee of the Storting.

Molotov: He is the Speaker of the Parliament.

Paasikivi: You may be assured that Sweden and Norway would not agree to conclude any aggressive alliance. Our new eastern frontier means a heavy concession on our part, but we strive in spite of that to bring about good relations with the USSR.

Molotov: For her part, the Soviet Union intends to observe the Peace Treaty. We are of the opinion that all questions between ourselves and Finland have been settled once for all. We now desire to work for the improvement of relations between our countries, holding fast, however, to the provisions of Article 3 of the Peace Treaty. The term "defensive alliance" alters nothing. The question is not solely of defense but also of an attack, of a military revenge. Nothing is said openly, to be sure, but the label of the alliance is not significant. From the very beginning, Tanner has spoken of securing the eastern frontier of Finland. Hambro, who as Speaker of the Foreign Relations Committee of the Storting exercises a considerable influence in Norwegian foreign policy, has said that the present eastern frontier of Finland is not permanent. How could it be changed? Solely by means of a war of revenge. We for our part immediately denied all statements alleging that we would not oppose a defensive alliance between Finland, Sweden and Norway. Hambro is not the only one who has spoken of the eastern frontier of Finland, for in Finland too the question of the eastern frontier is being written about. The contemplated alliance is in conflict not only with Article 3, but with the Peace Treaty as a whole. The purpose of the alliance has been disclosed by Hambro's statements, by Swedish activists, and by statements in the Finnish press.

Voionmaa: Sweden has not any aggressive designs. If Finland and Sweden attempt to come together in an alliance, this circumstance by itself guarantees the maintenance of peace along our borders.

Molotov: I do not agree. There is no unanimity of opinion in Sweden concerning her foreign policy. The present government of Sweden does observe neutrality, but there are other elements in Sweden which supported Sweden's participation in the war. Sandler is the leader of the group that favors war. To take part in the war would mean a great calamity for Sweden, but there are adventurers in Sweden who have lost control of themselves. Sweden may get a new government any day.

In the light of this, Sweden's participation in the alliance offers no guarantee that the alliance will be purely defensive. The label "defensive alliance" is not sufficient. We desire to state in advance, that if Finland becomes a member of the alliance in question, we can not remain indifferent.

Paasikivi: I do not remember whether there was any mention of the eastern boundary of Finland in connection with the defensive alliance. It should be kept in mind, however, that our other boundaries face Sweden and Norway. We have no common frontiers with any other state. If we conclude a defensive alliance with Sweden and Norway, it will not be aimed at the USSR, but at all states which intend to attack any state belonging to the alliance, be it Finland or Sweden or Norway. We are not at all thinking of revenge. Sweden and Norway would not be the right allies if we were to seek revenge. We should strive for an alliance with quite different states, if we really wanted revenge. Sweden and Norway are politically wholly defensive.

In this connection it should be pointed out that doubts are often expressed in Finland that the agreement with the USSR is not definitive, and that the USSR will present new demands to Finland. These suspicions make more difficult the activities of those circles in Finland which strive for a better understanding with the USSR. It is therefore important that the USSR should not act in a manner that keeps these suspicions alive. The defensive alliance aims at securing our future on the basis of the status quo.

Molotov: We are of the opinion that all questions between Russia and Finland have been settled, including the question of the security of Leningrad, Murmansk and the Murmansk Railway. Between us, therefore, there no longer are any questions in dispute. Your security is guaranteed by the nonaggression clause included in the Peace Treaty. If you conclude a defensive alliance with Sweden and Norway, we shall conclude that you have broken the Peace Treaty.

Paasikivi: You can not really believe that this alliance is directed against you.

Molotov: Hambro and others have disclosed its purpose.

Paasikivi: Hambro does not determine the foreign policy of the countries in question.

Molotov: Sandler and Hambro may tomorrow be members of the governments of Sweden and Norway.

Document 6

Telegram from the Finnish Legation in Moscow, Dated March 22, 1940

... Finally Molotov proceeded to discuss the question of the Finnish-Swedish-Norwegian defensive alliance. He referred several times to Hambro's speech, and to the disavowal by the Tass agency. He said that the USSR regarded the purpose of the defensive alliance as being revenge against the Soviet Union. The USSR also regards the defensive alliance as contrary to the Peace Treaty and our neutrality. A long conversation ensued, in the course of which we brought forward our contrary opinion, but he would not consent to give way. He assured us several times that the USSR will strictly observe the Peace Treaty.

J. K. PAASIKIVI
VÄINÖ VOIONMAA

Document 7

Extract from a Speech by Commissar Molotov, March 29, 1940

[*Helsinki Press,* March 30, 1940]

... Soviet Russia had the power to occupy all of Finland. We chose not to use it—something that no other Great Power would have done—and were satisfied with the least possible minimum. We must repel every attempt to violate the Peace Treaty recently concluded. Finland has made such attempts, and Norway and Sweden as well, using as a pretext a military defensive alliance. It is not difficult to understand that these efforts are directed against the USSR, and that their objective is to get satisfaction by avenging the war of 1939-1940. The participation of Norway and Sweden in an alliance with Finland would mean that these countries have abandoned their traditional policy of neutrality for a new foreign policy from which it would be impossible for the USSR not to draw the obvious conclusions.

Document 8

Minister Paasikivi's Letter to the Editor of the Pravda, May 7, 1940

To the Editor:

With reference to an article which appeared in the issue of your esteemed paper dated May 7 of this month (No. 126), entitled "How Obligations Are Observed," I beg respectfully to state that when these matters were discussed, I gave written notification on April 25 last, on behalf of the Finnish Government, that if, after the conclusion of peace, parts of industrial establishments located in territory ceded to the Soviet had either been moved to Finland or wrecked, they would be returned or compensation for them made.

J. K. Paasikivi,
Minister of Finland.

Document 9

Closing Section of a Finnish-language News Survey Broadcast over the Leningrad Radio on May 9, 1940, at 11 p.m.

... Finnish authorities broke the terms of the Peace. In the *Pravda* article published on May 7, incontrovertible facts were presented concerning barbaric destruction wrought after the conclusion of peace. The Soviet Union can not permit any kind of violations of treaty obligations, which the other contracting party has accepted in its relations to the Soviet Union.

Document 10

Memorandum Delivered by the Commissariat for Foreign Affairs to the Finnish Legation in Moscow on June 2, 1940

After the signature of the Peace Treaty on March 12 of the current year, while Finnish troops were being evacuated from Hanko, machinery and property belonging to harbor and defense installations, municipal and industrial enterprises, etc., were removed by Finnish action, and property in various places was destroyed.

The Soviet Government considers the measures mentioned, undertaken by Finnish authorities, as a violation of Article 4 of the Peace Treaty and demands the restoration of machinery and property removed from Hanko and compensation for property destroyed.

Appendix: List of removed and destroyed property, 3 pages.

Moscow, June 2, 1940

Document 11

Memorandum Delivered by Minister J. K. Paasikivi to Assistant Commissar for Foreign Affairs M. Dekanosov, June 8, 1940

MEMORANDUM

Concerning the Removal or Destruction of Machinery or Plant in the Territory Ceded to the Soviet Union

In its memorandum dated April 25, 1940, the Finnish Legation stated, on behalf of the Finnish Government, that if, after the conclusion of peace, any parts of industrial establishments had been removed from or destroyed in the territory ceded to the Soviet Union, they will be returned or compensation for them will be made.

This statement covers fully the obligation contained in Section 6 of the Protocol which is attached to the Peace Treaty. According to it, "the Army Commands of both Contracting Parties undertake, during the transfer of troops to the other side of the frontier, to take necessary measures, in the towns and localities to be ceded to the other Contracting Party, to preserve them from damage and to take necessary measures to preserve towns, localities, defensive and economic establishments (bridges, dams, aerodromes, barracks, depots, railway junctions, industrial establishments, the telegraph system, electric power stations) from damage and destruction."

This provision of the Peace Treaty means, that from the moment hostilities were closed—that is, beginning at twelve o'clock noon, Leningrad time, on March 13th last—and the transfer of the troops of the Contracting Parties began, the removal or destruction of any and all property within the meaning of Article 6 of the Protocol, in the territory ceded to the other Contracting Party, was forbidden, and the property in question was to be protected from damage and destruction.

On the other hand, the provision cannot of course apply to anything that had happened during the war, before the entry into force of the Peace Treaty.

In the Mixed Committee appointed to deal with this matter, the USSR delegates have nevertheless demanded that property removed or destroyed during the war, before the entry into force of the Peace Treaty, shall also be restored or compensation for it made.

The Finnish Government takes the view that this standpoint is not in harmony with the provisions of the Peace Treaty. During the peace negotiations, there was no mention of such an interpretation. It would therefore be essential that appropriate directions should be given to the USSR delegation in the Mixed Committee, to the effect that the moment at which Finland's obligation to restoration or compensation for property removed contrary to the provisions of Article 6 of the Protocol begins is, in conformity with the Peace Treaty, the entry into force of the Peace Treaty. This obligation will be scrupulously fulfilled by Finland. In order to bring about a speedy settlement in this matter, and in order that the USSR might speedily bring Enso into operation, a proposal was made on behalf of Finland in the Mixed Committee that all Enso machinery, enumerated in the list presented by the USSR, would be restored or compensated for, irrespective of when it was removed, on condition that other demands relating to this subject are withdrawn. To this proposal, however, the USSR delegation in the Mixed Committee refused to agree.

To aid in the settlement in the matter, the Finnish Government is prepared to restore, over and above the property covered by Article 6 of the Protocol appended to the Peace Treaty, in cases to be exactly defined, property which was removed before the entry into force of the Peace Treaty (in other words, property in respect of which no obligation of restoration exists under the Peace Treaty), provided that, in these cases, the USSR for its part agrees to a corresponding indemnity. If the USSR accepts this standpoint, the governments of both parties should issue directives to that effect to the delegations.

As it is especially desirable that a settlement should speedily be reached in this matter, we should be grateful, in the event that this proposal by Finland does not meet with the approval of the USSR, if the USSR would present a counterproposal on the basis of which a settlement satisfactory to both parties can be reached.

Moscow, May 31, 1940

Document 12

Memorandum Presented to M. Dekanosov by Minister J. K. Paasikivi, June 11, 1940

With reference to the memorandum of the Commissariat for Foreign Affairs, presented on June 2 to the Finnish Minister, relating to property removed from the Hanko area, the Finnish Legation has the honor, in accordance with instructions received, to present the following for the purpose of clarifying the Finnish standpoint in regard to the leased area, both in its theoretical and juridical aspects.

1. Article 6 of the Protocol attached to the Peace Treaty, which relates to measures pertaining to the transfer of troops *to the border of the Finnish state,* does not apply to Hanko, for its border is the border of *leased territory*. The provisions pertaining to cession of territory therefore do not apply to the Hanko lease area. Even the USSR admitted this, in that it did not refer, in its memorandum, to Article 6.

2. In Article 4 of the Peace Treaty, relating to the leasing of the Hanko area, no mention is made of the question now raised by the USSR, of property in the Hanko area; this area being only leased to the USSR. In the Peace Treaty there is, furthermore, no provision which limits the freedom of property owners to remove their own property. The conclusion is therefore natural, that an owner, irrespective of whether the owner is an individual, municipality, or the state, has the right, at least before the area was turned over to the USSR, to remove his property from the area.

3. In Finnish quarters no doubts whatever have been entertained regarding the freedom of action of owners in this respect. It has been assumed in Finland that in the USSR also the removal of property was regarded as a private concern of the Finns.

Before the act of turning over the area took place, a Soviet Commission of Officers arrived in Hanko on March 22. The Commission did not bring forward any new wishes in regard to the condition of the area when it was handed over. Neither were any remarks of this character made on the occasion when the territory was turned over to the USSR, at 12 P.M. on March 22. On this occasion, the USSR Commission that accepted the territory, noting that hoisting cranes were lacking in the harbor of Hanko, inquired whether Finland would be willing to sell them back.

4. In Article 4 of the Peace Treaty, the purpose of the leasing of Hanko is defined in terms of the establishment of a Soviet naval base in connection with which the USSR is granted the right to maintain adequate land and air forces in the area. On the other hand, there is no reference in the article to any economic objectives.

5. The conception prevailing in Finland of the property and other rights of the Finnish state and Finnish citizens in the leased Hanko area is disclosed by the proposal relating to Hanko, presented to the Commissar for Foreign Affairs by Professor Voionmaa and the present Finnish Minister at the meeting on March 21, 1940, of which a copy is appended hereto, and which was answered by the USSR in Clause 4 of the Memorandum of March 30, 1940.

The Finnish Legation begs for consideration of the above, which represents the view prevailing in Finland and shows that Finland has all along acted, in this matter, in good faith.

The Legation has the honor to add that even if removal of property from the Hanko area has taken place, property has in all likelihood not been destroyed, at least not on a scale to make it of any importance. In particular, there has been no destruction of military property.

In conclusion the Legation has the honor to inform you that the Finnish Ministry for Foreign Affairs has taken necessary steps to clear up the matter of the drawings and plans of the underground parts of the Hanko municipal telephone, electricity, sewer, and water supply, and other installations, and to forward these plans to the USSR authorities in the Hanko lease area, in accordance with the wish expressed by the Soviet Union.

Moscow, June 10, 1940

Document 13

Minutes of an Inquiry Conducted by Lieutenant-Colonel P. Waris by order of the Ministry of Communications with Reference to the Disaster to the Aircraft Kaleva. Governmental Secretary K. T. B. Koskenkylä and a German Subject, Gerhard Arnold Wilhelm Buschmann, were present

PARAGRAPH 1

Whereas the undersigned had made the acquaintance, in Helsinki, in May, 1941, of Herr Buschmann, who, in the course of conversation on other subjects, gave an eyewitness account of the destruction of the *Kaleva*, which I brought to the knowledge of the Ministry of Communications, the Ministry ordered the undersigned to carry out further inquiry into the matter.

PARAGRAPH 2

Herr Buschmann related the following: At the time when the *Kaleva* disaster occurred, I was director of gliding aeronautics in Tallinn. One of my glider pilots, Harald Mang, was serving his term of conscription at the Ker Lighthouse. The said Mang followed the course of events the whole time from the Ker Lighthouse with the aid of a powerful telescope, and he told me the following about it: "About 10-14 days before the destruction of the *Kaleva*, 1-2 submarines patrolled the route followed by the Helsinki-Tallinn air line from the Estonian coast to the middle of the Gulf of Finland. On June 14, 1940, I saw the *Kaleva* coming from the Estonian coast and two SB2 aircraft approach her from both sides, finally taking up positions about 50 meters distant from her. This 'formation flight' continued nearly up to Prangl, when one of the SB-2's descended lower, and immediately thereafter the machine gunner of the other aircraft, which had retained its position, rose into his machine-gun turret and fired his machine gun at the *Kaleva*, which was flying at the same height about 50 meters away on one side. The flight continued over Prangl, after this firing, for an estimated 2-3 nautical miles, after which the same SB-2 opened fire on the *Kaleva* a second time. The *Kaleva*, however, continued on her course at a height of about 400-500 meters. The SB-2 which had done the firing then descended lower, and the aircraft which had been flying on the other side of the *Kaleva* rose to a position beside the *Kaleva* on the opposite side, and when they were approximately above Ker, in turn opened fire on the *Kaleva*. A little while afterwards the left motor of the *Kaleva* stopped, smoke and flames began to appear, and banking to the left, the *Kaleva* plunged into the sea. In the vicinity of the scene of the disaster, some 3-4 nautical miles away, were some Estonian fishermen who hastened to the site in their motorboats, and began to collect various objects floating in the water. But soon a Russian submarine came on the scene, took the salvaged objects from the fishermen, drove them away, and continued the search by itself. One of the fishermen had hidden a leather portfolio belonging to a German passenger which the submarine crew had failed to find, and later handed it over to the Estonian frontier guard authorities at Ker. I kept a visiting card that had been in the portfolio as a memento. (Herr Buschmann could not remember the name on the card.) The same fisherman had salvaged a certain part of an aeroplane which I am unable to identify, but closely grouped bullet holes on it could clealy be seen."

Paragraph 3

The Board of Investigation had previously established that the cause of the disaster to the *Kaleva* was some outside factor, which, in the absence of adequate evidence, could not be defined with certitude. The above evidence, given under oath, proves that the conclusion of the Board of Investigation had been correct, and fully explains the destruction of the *Kaleva*.

Helsinki, July 1, 1941

On behalf of the Board of Investigation:

P. WARIS,
Lieutenant-Colonel, retired

Document 14

Telegram from the Finnish Legation in Moscow to the Ministry for Foreign Affairs, June 23, 1940

Commissar Molotov stated that Russia is interested in the Petsamo nickel resources, located not far from Russia, and asked whether we would grant the nickel concession to the Soviet Union, or agree to the establishment of a Finnish-Russian company, or make some other arrangement. I promised to report the matter to the government. I pointed out that the concession had been granted to an English corporation, and that we are probably legally bound in the matter, but that if we are free to act, we would be just as pleased to sell nickel to the Soviet Union as to others.

PAASIKIVI

Document 15

Telegram from the Finnish Legation in Moscow to the Ministry for Foreign Affairs, June 27, 1940

I call on Commissar Molotov in the Kremlin on June 27. I gave him a memorandum on the nickel question which had been drafted in co-operation with M. Gartz and Assistant Division Chief Jalanti. After reading it, Commissar Molotov said that it was not an answer to his question as to whether we would give them the concession, or form a joint company. I replied that the concession had been given to the British Canadian Corporation, but that we were trying to arrange the matter so that the USSR would be able to buy 50 per cent of the nickel ore. Commissar Molotov answered that they were not now interested in the ore, but in the area itself and the nickel in it, for all time, and that the British must be cleared out of the area. When I referred to the legal rights of the corporation, he replied that he was convinced that if the Finnish Government is desirous of annulling the concession given to the corporation, the corporation will raise no obstacles. An agreement can easily be reached with the Germans about the ore. He persisted in his proposal that the concession be canceled, and that we would thereupon come to an agreement with the USSR. Messrs. Kotilainen and Gartz will give an account of our negotiation.

PAASIKIVI

Document 16

Telegram from the Moscow Legation to the Ministry for Foreign Affairs on June 28, 1940

After I had finished my conversation with Commissar Molotov on June 27 about the nickel affair covered by my telegram,[1] I pointed out that the trade treaty was ready and should be signed before the departure of Kotilainen. Molotov answered that he wished first to take up the question of the Aaland Islands which Finland had fortified. The USSR attitude was now the same

---

[1] See Document 15.

as in the spring of last year, namely, that the Aaland Islands must not be fortified, but that if Finland wishes to fortify the Aaland Islands, fortification must be carried out jointly with the USSR, and on the basis of a joint agreement. The USSR also wishes to control that the Aaland Islands are unfortified, regarding all of which an agreement should be reached between Finland and the USSR. I remarked that this attitude differed from that expressed by Messrs. Stalin and Molotov last autumn, namely, that Finland may fortify the Aaland Islands if she does so alone. To this Molotov replied that the USSR had changed its attitude in this respect also since our last war, although he had not wished to take up the matter at the peace negotiations in order that no new difficulties might arise. When I pointed out that there was no connection between the Aaland Islands and the Petsamo nickel concession on the one hand and the trade treaty on the other, which could be signed now, Molotov answered that the USSR was prepared to conclude a trade treaty to help Finland, which is in a difficult position, and hoped that Finland for her part would arrange the Petsamo concession and the matter of the Aaland Islands to the satisfaction of the USSR. Kotilainen and Gartz will give an account of our negotiations.

Paasikivi

Document 17

Memorandum Presented by the Commissariat for Foreign Affairs to the Moscow Legation on July 6, 1940

With reference to the Memorandum of the Finnish Legation, dated June 11, relating to question of the restoration of plant and property removed from Hanko directly by the Finnish authorities themselves or with their permission, it is necessary to stress the following:

1. The USSR has been and still is of the view that according to Article 4 of the Peace Treaty, concluded on March 12, 1940, the USSR leases and takes under its administration from Finland not only the soil of Cape Hanko, with the waters and islands appertaining thereto, but expressly Cape Hanko with all the harbor and defense installations, municipal and industrial establishments, further the houses and buildings situated thereon, all of which, together, form an economic and defensive whole which can be directly used in the establishment of a USSR naval base.

2. As admitted by the Legation's memorandum, when Finnish troops were being transported from the area, not only property belonging to private individuals was removed and also destroyed, but also plant and property belonging to the Finnish state, and likewise plant intended for public use, with the result that the operation of the water supply, the telegraph service, the telephone service, lighthouses and other institutions (for instance, the hoisting

cranes mentioned in the Legation's memorandum were removed) has been disturbed.

3. In the memorandum of the Finnish delegation of March 21, not only is it admitted that the USSR authorities have the right to use all real estate belonging to the Finnish state, and situated in the Hanko area; it is further admitted that the USSR has the right to administer and use corresponding private property found in Hanko and essential to the military or administrative needs of the Soviet Union.

The memorandum of Commissariat for Foreign Affairs, dated March 30, 1941, which rejects the principle offered by Finland for compensating the evacuated inhabitants of the Hanko area at USSR expense, for losses sustained by them, contains a direct suggestion that Finland will leave the property in question in the Hanko area.

Thus the documents mentioned in the USSR memorandum, which relate to the cession of state-owned and even privately-owned property in Hanko that is essential for the establishment of the naval base, show that the stand of both Finland and of the Soviet Union is essentially the same.

4. The measures of Finnish authorities, in permitting the removal from the Hanko area of establishments and other property essential for the Soviet naval base, therefore mean a violation of the Peace Treaty concluded on March 12, 1940. The Finnish attempts to defend the measures in question must be considered as devoid of any justification.

The Government of the Soviet Union still demands that the plant, establishment and property removed from the Hanko area be returned, and that compensation be made for plant and property destroyed.

Moscow, July 6, 1940

Document 18

The Proposal for Hanko Transit Traffic Submitted by the Soviet Commissariat for Foreign Affairs on July 9, 1940: Extract from the Basis of the Proposal

According to Article 4 of the Peace Treaty concluded by the USSR and the Finnish Republic on March 12, 1940, the USSR has leased for 30 years the Hanko area and certain adjacent islands, in order to establish a naval base in the area.

In order to transport to the area the necessary land and air forces, the maintenance of which is presupposed by Article 4 of the treaty, and in order to supply the forces in question, it is essential that an agreement be made between the USSR and Finland whereby Soviet trains will be allowed to travel on Finnish railways to and from Hanko.

Document 19

Telegram from the Finnish Legation in Moscow to the Ministry for Foreign Affairs, dated July 10, 1940

After the discussion of consular problems, Secretary Sobolev unexpectedly delivered a memorandum. In it the Commissariat for Foreign Affairs states, after referring to our memorandum of June 26 prepared by Kotilainen, Gartz and Jalanti, that the USSR agrees to limit its 1940 purchases of nickel ore from Finland to 40 per cent, on condition that the rest of the ore is sold to Germany.

PAASIKIVI

Document 20

Memorandum Submitted by the Finnish Legation in Moscow to the Commissariat for Foreign Affairs on July 18, 1940

Referring to the memorandum of the Finnish Legation, dated June 11, 1940, and to possible later presentation of pertinent facts, the Finnish Government still holds that Finland is under no obligation to return property taken out of the Hanko area.

In view, however, of the fact that the Finnish Government desires to find a solution for this problem that will satisfy the USSR, it is hereby proposed that a Mixed Committee, composed of representatives of Finland and the USSR, be appointed. This Committee will prepare, for adoption by the Governments of Finland and the USSR, a proposal for the settlement of the matter in question which will be based upon the following principles:

(*a*) An estimate will be made of State and other public property which has been removed. The sum arrived at will be paid by Finland, either in cash or in kind.

(*b*) The proposal of the Mixed Committee will contain a detailed explanation of the property that belongs to each category.

(*c*) Private property will not be turned over, nor will compensation for such property be made, with the exception of possible exceptional cases, of which the Mixed Committee will likewise prepare a detailed proposal.

Document 21

Memorandum of the Commissariat for Foreign Affairs, Submitted to the Finnish Legation in Moscow on July 20, 1940

The Commissariat for Foreign Affairs hereby states, that it agrees to leave the handling of the question of the return of or the compensation for the establishments or other property removed from the Hanko area, to the Russo-Finnish Mixed Committee which functions at present in Viipuri. The principles proposed in Memorandum No. 204 of the Finnish Legation, dated July 18, 1940, will serve as the basis of the work.

Document 22

Telegram from the Finnish Legation in Moscow to the Ministry for Foreign Affairs, July 24, 1940

Commissar Molotov complained to me today that the members of the Finnish Government, especially Minister Tanner, oppose the work of the "Society for the Friendship and Peace between Finland and the USSR" (the SNS).

PAASIKIVI

Document 23

Telegram from the Finnish Legation in Moscow to the Foreign Ministry, August 4, 1940

When I called on Molotov about other matters on the third of this month, he again spoke of the persecution of the Society (SNS). I replied that one must not identify the work and objectives of the Society with the good relations between Finland and the Soviet Union. The people and the Government of Finland do strive for good relations. This is shown by the fact that things in general have been settled all right. The latest illustration of this is furnished by the Hanko railroad agreement, which was not mentioned at all in the Peace Treaty, and in which we agreed to a big concession. Molotov admitted that the Hanko railway matter was not mentioned in the Peace Treaty, but said that the transportation of Russian troops and material does not cause us any disadvantages. I replied to this that it is not pleasant to have the military of a foreign Power travel through our country. I said furthermore that the news of the Tass Agency is not correct, and that from the ranks of the Society shouting has been heard of bombings, which has left a very bad impression in Finland. M. Molotov insisted that such incidents were the work of nasty provocateurs. We agreed to discuss the matter after my return from Helsinki.

PAASIKIVI

Document 24

Treaty Proposal Concerning the Enso-Vallinkoski Rapids, Submitted by the USSR on August 16, 1940

Treaty for the Regulation of the Water Level of the Vuoksi River and for the Construction of the Enso Water Power Works

The Government of the USSR and the Government of Finland, being desirous of making arrangements for the regulation of the waters of the Vuoksi River, and for the solution of certain questions connected with the construction of the Enso Water Power Works, have designated as their Plenipotentiaries:

The Government of the Union of Soviet Socialist Republics............
....
The Government of the Republic of Finland............................
....

who, having exchanged their credentials, found in due and proper order, have agreed upon the following provisions:

Article 1

The Government of the USSR and the Government of Finland agree that the situation which existed in the regulation of the water of the Vuoksi River and of the Saimaa Lake, at the time of the signature of the Peace Treaty between the USSR and Finland on March 12, 1940, shall be considered as the normal condition in the regulation of the Vuoksi River. The raising of the waters of the Vuoksi River, presupposed by the plans for the construction of the Enso Water Power Works, shall not, however, be construed as being in violation of the normal regulation of the waters of this river.

Article 2

The Government of Finland may change the regulation of the waters of the Vuoksi River and Saimaa Lake, along that part of the River which lies within Finland's boundaries, only after every change has been the subject of an agreement with the Government of the USSR.

In addition to changing the water level in accordance with the plans for the completion of the Enso Water Power Works mentioned in Article 1, the USSR may effect changes in the regulation of the waters of the Vuoksi River along its course lying within Soviet territory, if such change cause damage or loss to Finland in the utilization of the river, only after each such change has been the subject of agreement with the Government of Finland.

Article 3

The Government of the USSR agrees to compensate, in part, the Government of Finland for the losses and expenses the Government of Finland will suffer or have to make as a result of the flooding of land in Finnish territory caused by the work of damming the Vuoksi in connection with the construction of the Enso Water Power Works.

The amounts to be paid by the Government of the USSR to the Government of Finland for the losses and expenses mentioned above, and the manner and time of payment, shall be established by a special agreement between the two Governments.

Article 4

Within two weeks of the going into effect of this treaty, the Government of Finland will turn over to the Government of the USSR, for its use:

1. The technical plans and drawings of the Enso Water Power Works;
2. A detailed list of the machinery which has been ordered for this Water Power Works (refers to turbines, generators, transformers, and electrical and other machines);
3. Certified copies of contracts, relating to the delivery of machinery for the Enso Water Power Works, entered into by the Enso-Gutzeit Company and Finnish and foreign firms.

Article 5

The Government of Finland will take necessary measures for transferring, in proper manner, to the construction organization of the Enso Water Power Works—in the event that the USSR desires it—all such delivery contracts, concluded by the Enso-Gutzeit Company and companies providing machinery, as will be considered essential for the completion of the Water Power Works. The Government of the USSR will make restoration for the advance payments made to such companies in accordance with the provisions of the delivery contracts.

Article 6

On the basis of a USSR proposal in the matter, the Government of Finland will undertake essential work, to be agreed upon in consultation with the USSR, for the regulation of the waters of the Vuoksi River and Saimaa Lake.

Article 7

This Treaty will go into effect immediately after it has been signed.

ARTICLE 8

This Treaty has been drawn up in a Finnish and a Russian copy, both of which are equally valid.

In witness whereof the representatives of the two Contracting Parties have affixed their signatures to this Treaty in Moscow.

.................., 1940

Document 25

Extract from the Speech of Prime Minister Risto Ryti, August 18, 1940 [1]

It followed, from the war and from the peace concluded at its close, that the establishment of relations with the Great Power that is our eastern neighbor has had a place all its own in the conduct of our foreign affairs.

The establishment of these relations with Russia is not limited to an endeavor merely to return to the relations that prevailed when the war began. It broadens into the deliberate attempt to build up relations that will guarantee friendly intercourse and peace, on a basis of mutual confidence and respect, between an independent, sovereign Finland and the USSR. We Finns are realists. We recognize existing facts and build on the foundation furnished by them. Thus we accepted the peace—once it was made—without reservations, despite the harshness of its provisions for Finland. It is on the basis of the peace that we proceeded to develop good neighborly relations.

The peace treaty itself presupposed, in its execution, a series of measures. Nearly all of them have by now been carried out. The new boundary has been fixed, and the documents pertaining to it ratified and ratifications exchanged. The marking of the boundary—that is, its marking in a physical sense—is about to be completed. Border incidents, which could not be avoided while the boundary was still indefinite, have come to an end. Peace along the frontier is complete. This is a circumstance of local as well as general significance.

Finland has returned, to Russia, property which had been removed, after the conclusion of peace, from industrial establishments in the areas ceded to the USSR. To be sure, differences of interpretation have risen as to whether the provisions of the Peace Treaty extended to the obligation to return property that had been removed. As was made public at the time, Finland has also for compensation turned over property which had been moved elsewhere already before the conclusion of peace. We understood that Russia needed this

---

[1] By August 1940, when this speech was made, the aggressive policy of the USSR had already been clearly revealed. The Prime Minister's speech was an attempt once again to reassure Russia that Finland was determined to do all in her power to maintain friendly relations, and carried the implication that the USSR should, in all reason, do the same.

property in order quickly to put into operation certain industrial establishments, and we wanted to help our neighbor in this effort. Even this good will and readiness of ours to help, show that the Government of Finland has tried in every way to further the development of friendly relations.

The exchange of prisoners of war, which the Peace Treaty contemplated, was carried out as rapidly as practical preparations permitted. The technical problems connected with the payments on the Hanko lease have been settled, and the USSR has already made the first payment. The commercial treaty contemplated by the Peace Treaty has gone into effect after the exchange of ratifications, and opens the door to brisk, mutual commercial exchange. The Salla Railway, which we are at present building as rapidly as possible, whose connecting railroad on the Russian side of the border is already finished, will conspicuously stimulate traffic between Finland and the Soviet Union. Of the measures connected with the Peace Treaty, mention should also be made of the fact that practical preparations are under way for the establishment of a Soviet consulate in Petsamo, where, because of the growing importance of the area, certain other consulates will also be opened.

In addition to measures that directly relate to the Peace Treaty, a number of arrangements have been agreed upon by Finland and the USSR, which are natural in the return to normal relations.

The telephone, mail and telegraph services between the two countries function again. The opening up of railway traffic has already been agreed to in principle. Finland has proposed that Russia should turn over certain archives in areas ceded to the Soviet Union, and the principle has been accepted by the USSR. Discussions of the extent to which archival materials should be returned are gradually progressing. Finland, on the other hand, has put at Russia's disposal scientific material dealing with the ceded areas.

I feel that special mention should be made of the good will shown by the Government of the USSR when it agreed to the return to Finland of the civilian population in the regions which had fallen into the hands of the USSR, thus recognizing the right of these people, who numbered about 2,000 souls, to live their own national life in their own way.

On the initiative of the Soviet Government, certain other questions, in which the USSR has informed us it is interested, have also been discussed. The Aaland question and the problem of transit traffic to the Hanko lease area belong in this category.

As regards the removal of troops and defenses from the Aaland Islands, the new arrangements mean a return to the status contemplated by the agreement of 1921, in force before the war, the signatories of which did not include the Soviet Union. The USSR has also expressed the wish that it be granted the right of transit traffic to the Hanko lease area. In principle, the Government of Finland has found it possible to agree even to this proposal. Negotiations for the organization of the transit traffic have not yet been completed. I therefore do not consider it appropriate, at this time, to go into details. Then there is the question of the return of property formerly in the Hanko lease area. Principles have been discussed, and agreement regarding them reached. A detailed proposal regarding the application of the principles will be formulated by the Mixed Commission.

As these illustrations indicate, various kinds of questions have been, and are, subjects of negotiation between Finland and the Soviet Union. They all point to a common end: the development of good-neighbor relations, and the solution, by means of negotiations and in a manner that will satisfy both countries, of the questions that have arisen. I have reviewed several of the concrete problems which have been dealt with in Finnish-Russian negotiations, in order to show how many different fields are involved in the re-establishment of relations between our two countries.

The questions that have come to the fore in the relations of the USSR and Finland do not involve only intercourse between the two Governments. Their many-sided character has led several groups of our citizens to participate, directly, in the effort to develop good-neighbor relations.

This relates, for instance, to economic co-operation, for which the commercial treaty recently concluded furnishes a good basis.

The two countries supplement one another in matters economic. We gladly buy products of the USSR, and for our part are in a position to furnish the Soviet Union with commodities it needs. Nothing is more natural or more to be desired than the further development of economic exchange between our two countries. If a secure foundation is now laid, the continuation of that development in the future will be guaranteed.

The same holds true of cultural co-operation. To foster it here in Finland, a special committee has been formed. We can only benefit from a knowledge of conditions in the Soviet Union, and it is our earnest hope that, while we for our part desire to learn about the cultural accomplishments of the Soviet Union, the USSR will also become familiar with the cultural conditions of our country.

Commissar Molotov stated, in his speech on August 1 of this year, that the development of the relations between the two countries depends on the Finnish Government. I have explained above the questions which have arisen between Finland and the USSR. In their handling, Finland has shown, in deed, her honest desire to strive, without prejudice, for the creation of best possible relations.

In the light of the concrete problems that have come to the fore, our honest policy of peace, supported by the Finnish people as a whole, stands revealed. We are also convinced that the USSR has the same aim. I have dwelt at length upon our relations with the Soviet Union, because the question is directly connected with the entire problem of our post-war reconstruction.

Document 26

Telegram from the Finnish Legation in Moscow to the Ministry for Foreign Affairs, August 22, 1940

After the Aaland matter, on August 22, I presented an explanation of the SNS on the basis of documents that I had received. Molotov listened and said that he doubted the correctness of our information. A lengthy discussion ensued which disclosed strong suspicion toward us. When I stated that in Finland there exists a general effort to establish good relations with the USSR, Molotov replied that the people desire it, to be sure, but the government's attitude is divided. It has been stated in our government circles, he claimed, that nobody who accepts the Peace of Moscow is a Finn. I said that it is impossible that such a statement could have been made, pointed to Prime Minister Ryti's speech, and to the fact that we have made arrangements for all the matters that have so far come. To this Molotov answered that unfortunately his contention was correct. He also claimed that we were hard at work on defenses in Hanko and along our border, and that hatred of the USSR is spread among the soldiers. I referred to my earlier statement concerning the duty of an independent state to look to its defenses, and I denied the stimulation of hatred among the soldiers. M. Molotov suggested that we are counting on some new turn, favorable to us, in the present Great War. I told him that this was the first time I had heard that thought expressed. Molotov stated that Tanner, in returning to the Elanto Co-operative, had only stepped behind the scenes. I pointed once again to Prime Minister Ryti's speech, whereupon M. Molotov said that the Prime Minister had side-stepped the main issue. In spite of my explanations, M. Molotov held on to his contentions, as he has ever done.

PAASIKIVI

Document 27

Telegram from the Finnish Legation in Moscow to the Ministry for Foreign Affairs, September 14, 1940

On September 13 I had a conversation with Commissar Molotov about the nickel affair. It was very disagreeable, as I had expected. I laid the matter before him in conformity with your telegram. Commissar Molotov replied that the sale of the output of nickel and the concession are two different things. The USSR wants the concession or a joint company. He said it depended on the Finnish Government whether or not the matter was arranged. Seeing that the Finnish Government had found it possible to allow a British-owned corporation to sell nickel to Germany, which was at war with Great Britain, it should not be impossible for the Finnish Government to arrange the concession question as well. When I emphasized the point that the government had no right to cancel the concession when the owners of the concession do not give their consent, he asked whether he was to understand the matter to mean that the Finnish Government is prepared to arrange the matter, provided a proper legal formula is found. This was possibly a hint that the USSR would be able to make arrangements with the British company. I answered that the representatives of the company had given us their final, negative answer, and that, as was known to Molotov from the company's report to the Sojusprom-export of August 17, the company has concluded an agreement with Farben.[1] I remarked that Germany too had wanted the concession and been given the same answer. When I pointed out that the company was prepared to conclude a long-term contract with the USSR for 40 per cent, Commissar Molotov replied that he did not want to negotiate with the nickel company but with the Finnish Government. He stressed that the USSR attached great importance to this matter, and regarded the granting of the concession to outsiders as being counter to the interests of the USSR. He added that the concession was also in conflict with both the 1920 and the 1940 Peace Treaties, as the USSR had been granted free transit through the very area in question. I protested against this interpretation, and brought forward all possible other arguments. He repeated, what he has said before, that it was not only the nickel that was important to the USSR, but the area itself, and that only Finland and the USSR were involved in the area. It appeared to me that our conversations and agreements with Germany were not to his liking. He said that this matter also again revealed the unfriendly attitude of the Finnish Government to the USSR, declaring that one could negotiate with Germany but not with Finland. Finally he asked me to lay the matter once more before the government, again emphasizing that the USSR attaches great importance to it.

PAASIKIVI

Document 28

Telegram from the Finnish Legation in Moscow to the Ministry for Foreign Affairs, September 28, 1940

Commissar Molotov stated on September 27 that they had heard that a secret treaty of alliance or pact exists between Finland and Sweden which is directed against the USSR and is in conflict with Article 3 of the Peace Treaty. I said that I could deny at once the existence of any such agreement. Molotov remarked that I was perhaps not *au courant* with events, but they possessed information. I asked the source of their information. Molotov was unwilling to disclose it, but said that hints had been made to the matter in Finland. He also made veiled hints about information received from Sweden. In this

---
[1] The agreement referred to was concluded between the Finnish Petsamo Nickel Company and I. G. Farbenindustrie.

connection, Molotov said that we were now talking verbally, but that if they brought forward documentary evidence, the matter would become grave.

PAASIKIVI

Document 29

Telegram from the Finnish Legation in Moscow to the Foreign Ministry, September 28, 1940

In regard to the size of the staff of the Aaland Consulate, I pointed out that there were twelve persons there now who could not have any work. We assume that the staff does not exceed the number of persons that may be considered reasonable. Molotov answered that if there was no work, the staff would be reduced.

PAASIKIVI

Document 30

Telegram from the Finnish Legation in Moscow to the Ministry for Foreign Affairs, September 29, 1940

Had a disagreeable conversation on September 27 with Commissar Molotov about Aaland Islands consultations, the Finland-Sweden alliance, German military transports, and the speeding up of the nickel affair. He pointed again to suspicions directed against us. Especially so long as the war continues, our position is dangerous and delicate. Molotov's words have contained veiled threats on several occasions, as will have appeared from my various telegrams.

PAASIKIVI

Document 31

Telegram from the Finnish Legation in Moscow to the Ministry for Foreign Affairs, October 1, 1940

Commissar Molotov invited me to the Kremlin on September 30 and said that it is impossible to accept our Article 4 in the Aaland Islands affair. First, because it does not include consultations, and secondly, because they cannot consent to the dispatch of notes all over Europe. He added, I believe in a spirit of derision, that perhaps France for example might not agree. He presented his final proposal in the matter of the Aaland Islands. Article 4 is left out altogether. I pointed out that the 1921 agreement remains in force, to which Molotov replied that it is immaterial to them how we interpret the continued validity or lapse of the 1921 agreement. In Article 2 they desire what had been left out of the 1921 agreement. I explained that we have regarded the part left out as unnecessary, but he paid no heed to that. Further, he made a strong demand that the agreement was to enter into force immediately on signature. He said that as the Peace Treaty went into effect at once, you can arrange this less important matter in the same way. Molotov was very angry and said that one cannot negotiate with you; this matter too remained open for months. With the Germans one can settle even big matters in a few days. He promised to give me later a written proposal, and demanded a solution of this question within one week.

PAASIKIVI

Document 32

Extract from Note No. 51 of the USSR Legation to the Ministry for Foreign Affairs, October 7, 1940

The plenipotentiary representation of the USSR demands unrestricted rights of travel for all officials of the USSR Consulate in Finland, in all areas included in the consular territory; the right for officials of the consulate to stay at their discretion in such areas, and to move about freely by any and all means of transportation in all parts of the consular territory.

The plenipotentiary representation expresses the wish that the authorities of the Republic of Finland will free the officials of the USSR consulates in Finland from any and all restrictions, and will create the best possible conditions to facilitate their work, and also give all necessary official aid to officials of the USSR consulates in the fulfillment of their official duties, and likewise that Finnish officials inform the plenipotentiary representation of the USSR to this effect.

Document 33

Telegram from the Finnish Legation in Moscow to the Ministry for Foreign Affairs, on October 10, 1940

I repeated on October 10, in the name of the government, that no alliance, agreement, or pact whatever exists between Finland and Sweden. Molotov said he took note of my statement.

PAASIKIVI

Document 34

Agreement Between Finland and the Soviet Union Concerning the Aaland Islands

The Government of the Republic of Finland, of the one part, and
The Government of the Union of Soviet Socialist Republics, of the other part, desiring to strengthen their security and foundations of peace in the Baltic Sea, have found it necessary to conclude among themselves the following agreement and have therefore appointed as their Plenipotentiaries:

The Government of the Republic of Finland:
The Envoy Extraordinary and Minister Plenipotentiary of Finland in Moscow, M. Juho Kusti Paasikivi;
The Government of the Union of Soviet Socialist Republics:
President of the Council of Commissars of the Union of Soviet Socialist Republics and Commissar for Foreign Affairs, Vjatsheslav Mihailovitsh Molotov,

who, having exchanged their credentials, found in due and proper order, have agreed upon the following provisions:

Article 1

Finland agrees to demilitarize the Aaland Islands, not to fortify them, and not to place them at the disposal of the armed forces of any other Powers.

This means also that neither Finland nor any other Powers can maintain or build in the area of the Aaland Islands any military or naval construction or base, no military air force construction or base, nor any other establishment for military purposes, and that the existing artillery foundations must be destroyed.

Article 2

The designation "the area of the Aaland Islands" means, in this Agreement, all the islands, banks and reefs located within the sea area bounded by the following lines:

a. To the north, north latitude 60° 41′.
b. To the east, straight lines, which consecutively join the following geographic points:

1) 60° 41′, 0 North lat. and 21° 00′, 0 East long.
2) 60° 35′, 9   "   "   "   21° 06′, 9   "   "
3) 60° 33′, 3   "   "   "   21° 08′, 6   "   "
4) 60° 15′, 8   "   "   "   21° 05′, 5   "   "
5) 60° 11′, 4   "   "   "   21° 00′, 4   "   "

6) 60° 09', 4 North lat. and 21° 01', 2 East long.
7) 60° 05', 5   "   "   "   21° 04', 3   "   "
8) 60° 01', 1   "   "   "   21° 11', 3   "   "
9) 59° 59', 0   "   "   "   21° 08', 3   "   "
10) 59° 53', 0   "   "   "   21° 20', 0   "   "
11) 59° 48', 5   "   "   "   21° 20', 0   "   "
12) 59° 27', 0   "   "   "   20° 46', 3   "   "

c. To the south, north latitude 59° 27'.

d. To the west, straight lines, which consecutively join the following geographic points:

13) 59° 27', 0 North lat. and 20° 09', 7 East long.
14) 59° 47', 8   "   "   "   19° 40', 0   "   "
15) 60° 11', 8   "   "   "   19° 05', 5   "   "
16) —the center of the Märket Rock
    60° 18', 4 North lat. and 19° 08', 5   "   "
17) 60° 41', 0   "   "   "   19° 14', 4   "   "

The territorial waters of the Aaland Islands are considered to extend three nautical miles from the islands, banks and reefs defined, above which rises the sea level, at least at times, at low water.

Article 3

The USSR is granted the right to maintain its own consular office in the Aaland Islands. In addition to ordinary consular functions, it shall also control the observance of the demilitarization and nonmilitarization of the Aaland Islands provided in Article 1.

In the event that the USSR consular representative observes circumstances which in his opinion run counter to the provisions of this agreement for the demilitarization and nonfortification of the Aaland Islands, he has the right to notify Finland's authorities, through the Provincial Government of the Aaland Province, of the holding of a joint investigation.

Such investigation will be conducted by a delegate of the Finnish Government and the USSR consular representative in the quickest possible manner.

The results of the joint investigation shall be recorded in a protocol drawn up in four copies in Finnish and Russian, and will be forwarded, for the purpose of undertaking necessary measures, to the governments of the two Contracting Parties.

Article 4

This agreement will go into effect immediately upon signature, and will thereafter be ratified.

Ratifications will be exchanged in Helsinki within ten days.

This agreement has been drafted in Finnish and Russian in two original copies.

Moscow, October 11, 1940

J. K. PAASIKIVI
V. MOLOTOV

Document 35

Minutes of the Finnish-Soviet Mixed Committee of October 19, 1940, Relating to the Surrender of Property Removed by Finnish Action from Hanko

Krogens, October 19, 1940.

Finland was represented by the chairman of the Finnish delegation Mr. Gräsbeck, the members of the delegation Wickström and Enckell, and a number of experts.

The USSR was represented by the chairman of the delegation, P. D. Orlov, and a number of experts.

At the session of the Mixed Committee, October 14-19, 1940, the list presented by the USSR of the machinery of all the state and public enterprises and establishments which had been situated on the peninsula of Hanko, was dealt with. Namely:

1. Postal service
2. Telegraph service
3. Telephone service
4. Wireless station
5. Public buildings
6. Hoisting cranes in the harbor
7. Refrigerating plant in the harbor
8. Lighthouses and machinery of the hydrographical establishments
9. Pumping station
10. Electric plant on the peninsula
11. Road and municipal administration
12. Railway service
13. Floating equipment and machinery of the harbor
14. Defense equipment

The plant of all the above-mentioned enterprises shall be restored by Finland in conformity with detailed and adjusted lists, in regard to which agreement has been reached between the two contracting parties, and which are in the possession of both parties.

Further in regard to the demand concerning defensive equipment, Finland has undertaken, in addition to that part of the equipment which is to be restored in kind, to pay compensation in cash for the rest of the equipment removed, and likewise the costs of repairing damaged equipment which the committee has assessed as 5,562,600 rubles.

Finland will present, on October 22, 1940, lists of the property belonging to the City Hall, the Municipal Hospital, and the Road Service of the peninsula, which is to be turned over.

In regard to the demand concerning railway transportation, the question of the quantity of rolling stock (locomotives and cars) to be turned over will be dealt with at subsequent meetings of the Mixed Committee, to be held in the city of Viipuri.

In addition to the lists of property belonging to the above-mentioned business enterprises and institutions, the committee also dealt with the lists of property belonging to the following private business enterprises:

   1. Manner's Machine Shop
   2. Meller's Automobile Repair Shop

The plants of these enterprises shall be turned over by Finland, also in conformity with lists in the possession of both parties.

All of the property mentioned, belonging to the institutions enumerated above, shall be surrendered by Finland to the USSR between the 25th day of October and the 20th day of November, 1940, at the Lappvik railway station.

These minutes have been drawn up in duplicate, in the Russian language.

      The Finnish delegation: W. GRÄSBECK
                J. WICKSTRÖM
                G. ENCKELL
   The Chairman of the USSR delegation: P. ORLOV

Note to the minutes of the Finnish-Soviet Mixed Committee, concerning the surrender of property removed from the peninsula of Hanko: In view of the fact that during the meetings of the Mixed Committee at Krogens between the 14th and 19th days of October, 1940, no agreement was reached in regard to the question of the surrender of railway rolling stock (locomotives and cars with spare parts), the Finnish delegation proposes that this question shall be left to a special committee, composed of representatives of Finland and the USSR.

Tammisaari, October 19, 1940

Document 36

Finnish Counterproposal to the USSR of November 1, 1940, in the Enso-Vallinkoski Matter

In the memorandum of the USSR concerning the Enso-Vallinkoski problem, which was handed to Finland at the end of last May, it is said:

"The USSR intends to complete the building of the Enso Power Station, in accordance with plans previously drawn up in Finland. As this plan presupposes the raising of the water level inside the banks of the Vuoksi River, in Finnish territory, and an alteration of Vuoksi River waters in the area adjacent to the frontier, the Soviet Government wishes to point out . . ."

Accordingly, and with reference to a proposal presented later by the USSR to Finland for an agreement relating to the regulation of the flow of the River Vuoksi, and the building of the Enso waterpower station, the USSR is requested to take into consideration the following Finnish views on the subject.

The USSR proposal for a draft agreement embodies a point of departure totally different from that proposed by Finland as a basis for negotiations. In the USSR memorandum, the Soviet Government is said to desire that the rights of *both parties* should be defined by agreement, and that the interests of *the USSR* and *Finland* in this matter be clarified. Finland embarked on negotiations on the basis formulated by the USSR, that the rights and interests of both parties would be clarified. An authoritative Finnish delegation, representing the highest possible degree of expert knowledge, gave the USSR authorities and experts in Moscow all the technical information they requested concerning the plan, so that the USSR now has a fully clear picture of what the question involves.

In the spirit of mutual confidence and striving for mutual understanding, which prevailed during these negotiations, the Finnish delegates laid before the USSR delegates, in the form of a memorandum, the general outlines (with factual explanations) which they regarded themselves as entitled to expect that the USSR draft agreement would follow. The Deputy of the Commissar for Foreign Trade, M. Stepanov, also officially stated during the negotiations that the USSR would deal with the matter in accordance with international law and the Peace Treaty. The Finnish delegation hoped that the USSR would show understanding in dealing with the Finnish point of departure, which, briefly repeated, is as follows:

The main height of fall is on the Finnish side of the border, and Finland can exploit it in the Vallinkoski Rapids by building a power station there at a cost of about 200 million marks which would provide Finland with about 500 million kwh. If interest and amortization, etc., is calculated at 10 per cent, and the value of the current sold at the station at 10 penni per kwh., the annual expenditure is 20 million marks, which corresponds to the receipts from 200 million kwh., leaving a net surplus of 300 million kwh. per year. It should be observed, however, that as soon as the power station has been amortized, which would in all likelihood be the case after a very brief period, seeing that the price of current reveals, for many reasons, an upward tendency in Finland, nearly the whole of the energy generated by the power station, approximately 500 million kwh., is clear profit (except for insignificant maintenance costs).

Finland is under no obligation to surrender this asset, either in international law or under the terms of the Peace Treaty. Nevertheless, appreciating that intimate co-operation between two neighbors should be possible in reaching a settlement satisfactory to both parties in a matter of this kind, the Finnish delegation deemed it possible to come to an arrangement whereby Finland would cede to the USSR the right to raise by damming the water level in the River Vuoksi on the Finnish side of the frontier in a manner to be defined later, and thus place at the disposal of the Enso power station the fall on the Finnish side of the boundary. In return for this water power, the USSR would annually furnish to Finland 300 million kwh. or 45 per cent of the capacity of the Enso-Vallinkoski power station. Even this proposal meant, in the light of the above, an appreciable sacrifice on the part of Finland, namely the loss, after the elapse of the time needed to amortize Finland's own power station, of about 200 million kwh. annually or ($200 \times 100/500/$) 40 per cent of the water power belonging to her. As an additional concession the Finnish delegation proposed that Finland would carry out, at her own expense, the clearing of the Kyyrönkoski Rapids, and would undertake to pay the compensation for damage to shores on her own side of the frontier, and to construct the necessary communications, including bridges. In concluding the agreement, Finland is compelled to take care that no loss is caused to the Imatra power station by the damming. A clause relating to this question was proposed for inclusion in the agreement.

As will have appeared from the above, the lines of policy proposed by the Finnish delegation were drawn up in accordance with economic principles. In other words, they embodied the idea that one party was conceding something (Finland, water power) and the other party compensating it for the concession (the USSR furnishing electrical current).

The first draft proposal of the USSR meanwhile starts out from the standpoint that Finland is to surrender to the USSR the water power of the Vallinkoski Rapids, without receiving anything in return. As no reasonable explanations or elucidations are appended to the draft agreement, it is difficult for Finland to understand what principle the USSR has followed in arriving at such a proposal. In Finland's view, no basis can be found for the USSR proposal either in international law or in the Peace Treaty.

As Finland still desires to believe that a joint basis can be found for negotiation along the lines proposed by Finland, the draft agreement below has been drawn up in conformity with those lines.

AGREEMENT

relating to the regulation of the water level in the Vuoksi River in the immediate vicinity of the frontier between the Republic of Finland and the USSR and to the building and operation of the Enso water power station.

The Government of the Republic of Finland and the Government of the USSR, being desirous of arranging by agreement the water level in the Vuoksi River in the immediate vicinity of the frontier between Finland and the USSR, together with certain other questions connected with the building and operation of the contemplated Enso water power station, and of defining in these matters the rights and obligations of both parties, have for that purpose appointed as their plenipotentiaries:

The Government of the Republic of Finland..............................

....

The Government of the Union of Soviet Socialist Republics.................

....

who, having exchanged their credentials, found in good and due form, have agreed upon the following provisions:

Article 1

The Government of the Republic of Finland guarantees that the average daily flow of the Vuoksi River in the present state of the flow will not be changed.

The Government of the USSR, for its part, guarantees that the water level in the Vuoksi River on the Finnish side of the frontier will not be raised by damming on the USSR side of the border except for the special case mentioned in Article 2.

Article 2

The Government of the Republic of Finland grants to the Government of the USSR the right, subject to the compensation defined in Article 3 below, to dam waters in the water power station to be built at Enso, in the part of the Vuoksi River which is on the USSR side of the frontier, to the level defined in the damming regulations appended to this agreement. The Government of the USSR undertakes to arrange and manage the damming operations intended by the present article with special regard to the avoidance of damage to the Imatra water power station, or to other Finnish interests in the utilization of the flow of the Vuoksi.

Article 3

In compensation for the height of fall surrendered for utilization by the Enso power station, and for the corresponding water power, the USSR will supply Finland annually with electrical energy averaging 300 million kwh. of 120 kw. tension, or more specifically will continuously supply 45 per cent of the energy developed by the Enso-Vallinkoski power station at each state of the flow. The supply of electrical energy to Finland will begin immediately after the power station has been completed to the point where it, or a part of it, is put into operation.

The technical details of the supply of electrical energy will be agreed to separately.

Article 4

Finland undertakes to carry out, at her own expense, the clearing of the Kyyrönkoski Rapids, in accordance with the damming regulations mentioned in Article 2. The clearing is to be carried to a conclusion within two years of the entry into force of this agreement. Finland also undertakes to pay compensation for damage to shore property caused on her own side of the frontier by the damming operations, and to construct the road communications, including bridges made necessary by the damming operations.

Article 5

As compensation for the building plans and drawings for the Enso water power station, for the specifications of the machinery ordered which the Enso-Gutzeit Company has already made over to the USSR, and for the costs incurred by the Enso-Gutzeit Company in connection with contracts, the Government of the USSR undertakes to pay to the Enso-Gutzeit Company, through the Government of the Republic of Finland, the sum of 7,000,000 marks within one month of the entry into force of this agreement.

Article 6

The Government of the Republic of Finland will take measures to see that the Enso-Gutzeit Company, for its part, will transfer, upon the request of the Government of the USSR, freeing itself from all future liability, the contracts concluded by it for the Enso power station and that are still valid, to the Enso power station building organization, provided that, on the entry into force of this agreement, no other arrangement has been made between the USSR authorities and the contractors in regard to the said contracts.

The Government of the USSR will reimburse the Enso-Gutzeit Company for advance payments paid by the said company to contractors in respect of both the contracts to be transferred under Paragraph 1 of this Article, and the contracts becoming invalid as a result of new contracts concluded by USSR authorities and the contractors.

Article 7

This agreement shall be ratified. The instruments of ratification shall be exchanged in Helsinki at the earliest possible date.

The agreement shall go into effect on the exchange of instruments of ratification.

This agreement has been drawn up in duplicate original copies, in Finnish and in Russian. Both texts are equally valid.

In witness whereof the plenipotentiaries of the two Contracting Parties have affixed their signatures to the present Agreement.

Moscow, ...

Document 37

Telegram from the Moscow Legation to the Ministry for Foreign Affairs, October 30, 1940

After the Aaland Island affair, Assistant Commissar for Foreign Affairs Vyshinski said that he had a grave matter to discuss: The Petsamo nickel concession, a matter which the Finnish Government has been delaying for months. He had in front of him the same notes as Molotov had had. He referred to the notification made by Ambassador Cripps and said that the Finnish Government could arrange the matter, but did not wish to do so, and was using pretexts. I answered that the nickel company had given a written categorical refusal, and that the British Minister in Helsinki had quite recently reported that Great Britain did not want the concession to be transferred. In the circumstances we can do nothing in the concession matter. I suggested a long-term contract to deliver nickel. To my remark that we could not take away the concession from the British, M. Vyshinski replied by asking whether Finland was a British colony. The USSR has regarded Finland as an independent state, and wishes to respect her independence. He asked if it was our final reply, adding that in that case the USSR would be compelled to take the measures which the situation demanded. A long conversation ensued on the subject, and M. Vyshinski asked me to give the final answer of the Finnish Government in two or three days. He regarded the matter of deliveries as something apart from the concession. I promised to return to the subject in two or three days. It is my impression that the USSR will not drop the matter.

PAASIKIVI

Document 38

Telegram from the Ministry for Foreign Affairs to the Moscow Legation, October 31, 1940

Prime Minister Ryti declared to Zotov (will you notify Vyshinski to the same effect): "We have not postponed the nickel affair in order to plan what to do next, but because we have not been able to come to an agreement with the nickel company. As a state based on law we honor our agreements. The attitude adopted by the USSR brings us into conflict with Great Britain and even with Germany. We agree to the transfer of the concession to a Finnish-Russian company on condition that the USSR procures the consent of Great Britain and the nickel company, and the withdrawal by Germany of the request she made for the concession before the USSR." Zotov asked whether they might inform the British and Germans that Finland wished for such a solution. Prime Minister Ryti said: "We wish that the situation would remain unchanged until the end of the war, but the USSR may say that Finland consents if Great Britain and Germany consent."

Document 39

Note No. 63 of the Soviet Legation, to the Ministry for Foreign Affairs, November 2, 1940

The plenipotentiary representation of the Union of Socialist Soviet Republics in Finland has the honor to inform the Ministry for Foreign Affairs of the Republic of Finland of the following: (1) The facts brought forward in the note of the plenipotentiary representation of the Soviet Union of October 7, and its memorandum of October 9, show that the Finnish authorities have applied a veritable system of obstacles to officials of the USSR consulates. These measures by Finnish authorities are designed to restrict the activities of the USSR consular representatives and their character is in conflict with Article 6 of the Peace Treaty concluded on March 12, 1940, between the USSR and the Republic of Finland, and Article 3 of the agreement relating to the demilitarization and nonfortification of the Aaland Islands concluded between the USSR and Finland on October 11, 1940, which define the duties of USSR consulates in Finnish territory.

The statement by the Ministry for Foreign Affairs on October 25 of this year, in which the measures of the Finnish authorities are found to be correct with regard to the facts brought forward in the above-mentioned note and memorandum of the plenipotentiary representative, must be considered as evidencing lack of desire on the part of the authorities of the Finnish Republic to create favorable conditions for officials of the USSR consulates in Finland. This is proved by the circular note of the Ministry for Foreign Affairs No. 25088 of October 25, which limits the rights of the USSR consulates in Finland. (2) The plenipotentiary representation of the USSR cannot accept the travel regulations for officials of the USSR representatives in Finland, contained in the circular note of the Ministry for Foreign Affairs No. 25088 of October 25, and continues to adhere to its demand that: (*a*) the officials of the Petsamo and Mariehamn consulates shall be granted unlimited freedom of movement by any and every means of transport within the territories falling within the jurisdiction of the consulates, and the City of Helsinki, and the right to stay in any locality within their consular district. The same opportunities shall be provided for officials of the commercial representation in Petsamo. That, (*b*) the officials of the plenipotentiary and commercial representations shall be granted the right of unrestricted travel and departure from the consular districts by any means of travel, and the right to stay in any locality in the consular district. That, (*c*) newly appointed officials of the USSR consulate and commercial staffs in Petsamo shall be granted the right to travel to the consular district on the basis of permits to enter the country issued by the Finnish Legation in Moscow. That, (*d*) the Ministry for Foreign Affairs, in the event that a permit issued by Finnish authorities is needed for the rights mentioned under (*a*) and (*b*) of Clause 2, will kindly at once grant such permits, valid for one year.

Helsinki, November 2, 1940

Document 40

Telegram from the Moscow Legation to the Ministry for Foreign Affairs, November 2, 1940

On November 1 took up in the Commissariat for Foreign Affairs the question of the ownership of the Vallinkoski Rapid and presented our counterproposal. I pointed out that the question of ownership must be settled in principle, after which the experts can do the rest. When I remarked that Finland's property rights in Vallinkoski are clear, and that we cannot accept the USSR proposal, Molotov angrily replied that Finland has not revealed any desire to discuss economic matters with the USSR in a reasonable spirit, thus hinting also at the nickel question.

PAASIKIVI

Document 41

Telegram from the Moscow Legation to the Ministry for Foreign Affairs, November 2, 1940

Commissar Molotov invited the undersigned to see him in the Kremlin on November 1. He was in a very angry mood. He said that the Finnish Government does not wish to discuss economic matters with the USSR in a reasonable spirit, and at the same time hatred of the USSR is being fanned in Finland. He took up first the nickel concession, and sternly complained of the delay. He demanded an answer to the question whether the Finnish Government is willing to negotiate in the matter of the concession, if the nickel company gives its consent. He referred again to the statement by Ambassador Cripps. I gave the same answer as to Vyshinski the day before yesterday. Commissar Molotov also hinted that the USSR would proceed to action if the matter is not arranged. He did not mention the nature of the measures. He said that the USSR must also receive, this year, 40 per cent of the ore as agreed. I answered that to my knowledge the mines were not yet working, to which Molotov replied: "And yet you do not want us to help."

PAASIKIVI

Document 42

Telegram from the Moscow Legation to the Ministry for Foreign Affairs, November 6, 1940

On November 5 I notified Vyshinski of the contents of your telegram of October 31 regarding nickel. Vyshinski said he had spoken with Ambassador Cripps, who, disavowing Minister Vereker, confirmed what he had told Commissar Molotov in July, but to the effect that the nickel company was prepared temporarily to transfer the concession up to the end of the war. Commissar Vyshinski took the view that this condition was of no significance, and that the matter was settled with the British. He said that the Germans had reported already earlier that they did not want the concession, but would be satisfied with 60 per cent of the nickel, and therefore there was no further need to take up the matter with them. He was of the opinion that the Finnish Government could now unilaterally annul the concession, after which, as the owner of the mines, the Finnish Government could do as it pleased. I answered that, according to our laws, the consent of the nickel company was needed for an annulment of the concession, and that the condition as to time, now brought forward by Ambassador Cripps, would have to be withdrawn, as the concession agreement with the company would have to be definitely annulled.

PAASIKIVI

Document 43

Telegram from the London Legation to the Ministry for Foreign Affairs, November 7, 1940

I notified Mr. Collier today of your telegram 632. Mr. Collier assured me that Ambassador Cripps had never been sent any other directives than those reported by Minister Vereker. . . . He said we could inform the USSR that the matter will not be settled with the British until the USSR undertakes not to export any nickel to Germany. This is a condition for any settlement which Great Britain would approve. He added that he would inform me later whether they could give the written notification you asked for.

GRIPENBERG

Document 44

Telegram from the Moscow Legation to the Ministry for Foreign Affairs, November 12, 1940

I was to see Vyshinski on November 12, about the nickel affair. I brought forward that we had asked the British Government whether it was prepared to give us its written consent, on its own behalf and on behalf of the company, to the transfer of the concession without a time limit, and that we had received the answer that the question had not yet been settled and that the British would inform us later. I asked that the USSR would arrange matters both with the British and the Germans, after which we were ready to negotiate at once regarding a mixed company. Vyshinski replied that the USSR would no longer open negotiations either with the British or the Germans. It is in the power of the Finnish Government to arrange the matter, if we only wish, and conversations with Great Britain are a matter for Finland and not for the USSR, as the question concerns the territory of an independent Finland. In his opinion, we could simply inform the British Government that we are annulling the concession with a view to other arrangements. If we fail to do so, the USSR will regard it as a refusal. A long conversation ensued. I pointed out that under our laws we could not take away the concession from the British. Vyshinski paid no attention to my explanations about conceptions of law in the northern countries, but answered that if the requisite law did not now exist, we could go ahead and pass one. For this, he held, only good will was needed. He asked for an answer in the near future, the matter having been so long delayed. He referred privately, as he put it, to the fact that the USSR could have retained Petsamo in the peace of 1920, and in the peace of 1940.

PAASIKIVI

Document 45

Extract from a Memorandum Presented by the Soviet Legation to the Ministry for Foreign Affairs on November 19, 1940

The plenipotentiary representation of the USSR would be obliged to the Ministry for Foreign Affairs if it would kindly arrange permits for a year for:
1. The officials of the USSR consulate and subsection of the commercial representation at Petsamo, and the officials of the USSR plenipotentiary and commercial representations (according to a list) for unrestricted travel in the entire province of Lapland, in accordance with the rules presented in the note of the USSR plenipotentiary representations of July 30, and the note of the Ministry for Foreign Affairs of August 2, using all means of travel (railway, automobile, aircraft, on foot, under water, etc.) and on all travel routes (railways, waterways, highways, of national or local significance), in all directions,

and also the right to stay freely in populated areas and to travel to and from Helsinki;

2. The officials of the USSR plenipotentiary representation (according to a list) for unrestricted travel by all means of travel to any locality in the Aaland Islands, for visits to the Islands, and also for stays thereon.

Document 46

Telegram from the Moscow Legation to the Ministry for Foreign Affairs, November 20, 1940

Commissar Molotov invited me on November 19 to the Kremlin, and said that he had had talks in Berlin about the nickel. He told me that Germany withdrew from the concession and had no objection to the transfer of the concession to the USSR. Germany was interested in delivery of nickel, Commissar Molotov remarked about our agreement with Farbenindustrie. He regarded Great Britain's temporary consent as adequate; the Finnish Government can therefore decide the matter at once. He demanded that the matter should at last be settled. I answered that I had pointed out all along that the unconditional consent of Great Britain and the nickel company was essential. Great Britain had consented on condition Germany receives no nickel. I said that I had understood Molotov to accept our standpoint that the consent of the nickel company was needed. Molotov replied that that was a misconception; "You have always spoken about the consent of the company, but I have not approved that standpoint." He said that we must arrange the question in one way or another. With reference to the British condition that no nickel was to go to Germany, Molotov said: "Sell all the nickel to the USSR, which will take care of the matter." I understood that the USSR would give Germany her share. Molotov demanded in an insistent tone that the nickel affair be settled without delay. I informed him that I had notified my government of my conversation with Vyshinski on November 12, and was awaiting a reply. I promised an answer in a few days' time.

PAASIKIVI

Document 47

Note of the Ministry for Foreign Affairs No. 26421 to the USSR Legation on November 21, 1940

With reference to the USSR Legation's note No. 63 of November 21, 1940, the Ministry for Foreign Affairs has the honor to bring to the notice of the USSR Legation the following:

As will appear from the Ministry for Foreign Affairs' circular note of October 25 last, the restrictions on travel in force in Finland are general and the same not only for Finnish nationals but for all representatives of Foreign Powers. They do not in any way or at any point discriminate against the representatives of the USSR in regard to freedom of movement, as compared with the representatives in Finland of other Foreign Powers. As regards the freedom of movement of officials of the USSR Consulate in Mariehamn, within the consular territory, the Ministry for Foreign Affairs notes, at the same time referring to its above-mentioned circular note, that officials of the said consulate may without special travel permits, but furnished with appropriate evidence of their identity, move about within the whole province of Aaland. Similarly officials of the said consulate may, without special permission, travel from their consular territory to Helsinki provided they do not pass through a prohibited area, of which, however, there are none on the direct route. On their return journey, however, they must carry a regular travel permit to be shown to the control authorities. Such permits can be obtained from the political police through the Ministry for Foreign Affairs, or the Governor of the Province of Aaland, and are granted for a period of three months at a time.

A corresponding freedom of movement is in force in regard to officials of the Petsamo consulate within the Petsamo police district, with the exception of the Liinahamari and Trifona harbor areas, where movement is prohibited for reasons of safety. In regard to movement in these two areas, the representatives of the political police in Petsamo will grant permission, which, if travel there is regarded as justified, is obtainable without delay on due application. Up to the present, also officials of the USSR consulate in Petsamo wishing to travel outside of the Petsamo police district to other areas belonging to the consular territory have been required to procure a travel permit, because the journey southward from the said police district means passing through a prohibited area (the Inari police district). In order to go as far as possible, however, toward meeting the wishes expressed by the USSR Legation, and being desirous of facilitating further the activities of the consulate and commercial representation in Petsamo, the proper Finnish authorities have now removed this restriction, so that officials of the consulate and commercial representation may now travel from the Petsamo police district, by the main highway (No. 4), via Ivalo in the Inari police district, to Rovaniemi, and by the same route back from Rovaniemi without a travel permit granted separately for each journey. The representative of the political police in Petsamo, who is to be given the necessary instruction and whom the Petsamo consulate will kindly approach in due time, will issue to officials of the consulate and commercial representation in Petsamo a travel permit of this character, valid for three months at a time.

Similar travel permits, valid for three months, will be granted also to persons belonging to the official staff of the USSR Legation. The Ministry for

Foreign Affairs has already received from the Legation, for this purpose, certain lists of persons for whom the Legation desires travel permits valid for a specific period. The Ministry for Foreign Affairs will, in a few days—after having been in communication with the Legation, in case of need, regarding details—give its answer as to which of the persons enumerated in the lists it will be necessary to provide with the permits in question.

As regards other travel permits, the greatest good-will will be shown in the granting of these, *in casu,* on the basis of the system in force. On the other hand Finnish authorities regret that they cannot see their way to consenting to the adoption of the season travel permits suggested in the note. Season permits of this description have not been granted to Legations of other Foreign Powers in Finland, nor have such been requested.

In clause 2-C it is proposed that newly appointed officials of the USSR consulate and commercial representation in Petsamo should be granted the right to travel from Helsinki to the place of their duties with permits to enter Finland issued by the Finnish Legation in Moscow, and in clause 2-D, that diplomatic couriers should be granted the right to travel to the USSR consulates in Petsamo and Mariehamn, similarly with permits to enter the country issued by the Finnish Legation in Moscow. It is impossible for the Finnish Legation in Moscow, which is entitled to issue only permits to enter Finland, to grant, under the system in force, the right implied by the request of the USSR Legation, which is expressly reserved to the political police; to effect an alteration in this respect would require a fundamental change in the entire, extensive system of travel regulations. Moreover, there is no material reason for an alteration of the system, as travel permits to USSR consulates situated in prohibited areas can be arranged without delay in other ways. In the granting of these permits, there is no delay, and they are granted at the earliest opportunity on request by the Legation through the Ministry.

By the above alleviations within the framework of the system in force, it is desired to relieve, to the greatest possible extent, persons belonging to the USSR representations from the difficulties which the USSR Legation regards the formalities connected with the present system as causing. The Ministry for Foreign Affairs expresses the hope that the manner in which the matter is handled in practice, will meet the wishes of the USSR Legation.

Document 48

Extract from note No. 26400 of the Ministry for Foreign Affairs to the USSR Legation, on November 21, 1940

Similarly Minister Zotov, while traveling to Petsamo at the end of September, acted in a manner which did not correspond with what had been agreed upon regarding his journey before it was undertaken. The Counselor of the

USSR Legation, Jelisejev, in a memorandum handed by him on the 19th of this month to Minister Voionmaa, Secretary General of the Ministry for Foreign Affairs, has called to mind the incident in question. According to M. Jelisejev, Finnish authorities had stopped Minister Zotov's car, "in spite of permits, identification documents and passport that had been presented." The Ministry wishes, with reference to this matter, to present the following. In spite of the fact that regular air traffic to Petsamo had been suspended, a special airplane was provided for Minister Zotov's journey to Petsamo and back. It was also expressly set down on Minister Zotov's travel permit, that the journey would be made by air. This notwithstanding, Zotov set out on his return journey by car, without informing the authorities that he was going to do so. Thus, when the car was halted en route, the reason was solely the circumstance that Minister Zotov's travel permit lacked the proper entry which would have entitled him to proceed, by car, through prohibited areas.

The Ministry expresses the sincere desire that members of the USSR representation would carry, while traveling in Finland, the necessary identification documents, and that they would accept in a spirit of understanding the regulations and formalities in force in regard to travel. By doing so they would be contributing to our mutual advantage, to the creation and maintenance of good relations with the Finnish control authorities, and at the same time ease the efforts of the Foreign Ministry to make it possible for the staff of the USSR representation to travel as freely as possible, within the framework of the general travel regulations.

Document 49

Information about the Salla Railway, given by the Minister for Foreign Affairs, M. Witting, to Minister Zotov on December 3, 1940

The Ministry for Foreign Affairs has received the following information about the present stage of construction of the Kemijärvi-Salla Railway:

1. Thirty-three kilometers of railway bed is ready for laying of rails; 345,000 cubic meters of material has been removed from cuttings.

2. Cuts and embankments are being constructed along a distance of 53 kilometers. In this section 1,000,000 cubic meters of earth still remain to be transported away. The total length of the railway line is 86.5 kilometers.

3. Ten bridges are under construction: the foundations of two ground supports are ready, and supports are under construction for bridges; concrete is being laid for one support; for three supports, foundation pits have been dug; for seven ground supports and pillars, foundation pits are being dug; twelve culverts have been built.

4. The laying of the rails will take three months.

5. During the past three months, wages have been paid fortnightly to the

following number of workers: August 31, 1,361 men; September 15, 1,488 men; September 30, 1,627 men; October 15, 1,707 men; October 31, 1,838 men; November 15, 2,164 men.

6. Next winter 2,000-2,500 workers will be employed.

Document 50

Telegram from the Moscow Legation to the Ministry for Foreign Affairs, December 7, 1940

Commissar Molotov invited me to the Kremlin at half past twelve midnight on December 6, and said that he had two statements to make. He read them from a paper which, at my request, he gave to me. One of them ran as follows:

The Soviet Government has received from its Minister in Stockholm, Madame Kollontay, information given to her by Foreign Minister Günther and the Finnish Minister Wasastjerna, that an agreement is under preparation between Sweden and Finland, for the subordination of Finland's foreign policy to Stockholm, and that henceforth the foreign policy of Finland will not be directed from Helsinki, but from Stockholm. The Soviet Government takes the view that such a situation, were it actually to come into being in relations between Helsinki and Stockholm, would denote the liquidation of the Peace Treaty concluded between the USSR and Finland on March 12, 1940, according to which the party contracting with the USSR is not a Finland in a state of vassalage, unable to assume responsibility for the fulfillment of the treaty, but a sovereign Finnish state which has its own foreign policy and is able to discharge responsibility for the obligations assumed by it in the treaty.

"The Soviet Government advises Finland to weigh what has been said above, and to consider the consequences which an agreement of this kind, concluded by Finland with any foreign state, Sweden not excepted, will bring!"

PAASIKIVI

Document 51

Telegram from the Moscow Legation to the Ministry for Foreign Affairs, December 7, 1940

The second statement made by Commissar Molotov on December 6, was as follows: "We do not wish to interfere in the matter, or make any hints with reference to the nominations for a new presidential candidate in Finland, but we are watching closely the preparations for the election. We shall conclude whether Finland desires peace with the USSR, on the basis of who is chosen as President. It is clear that if some such person as Tanner, Kivimäki, Mannerheim or Svinhufvud is elected President, we shall draw the conclusion that

Finland does not wish to observe the Peace Treaty she has concluded with the USSR." I remarked that the election of a President was a purely domestic affair of ours, which Molotov admitted. He added that of course you can elect whomever you like to the presidency, but we have the right to draw our own conclusions. I said that we will observe the peace treaty; the presidential election does not affect that. As Molotov read the above from his paper, I could not help listening, and at my request he gave me the paper. I bring the matter hereby to your attention.

PAASIKIVI

Document 52

Note No. 77 presented by Minister Zotov to Minister of Foreign Affairs, M. Witting, on December 10, 1940

YOUR EXCELLENCY:

I have the honor to call your attention to the following: In spite of several conversations with you and corresponding representations to the Ministry for Foreign Affairs, concerning greater freedom of movement for officials of the Petsamo consulate and of the subsection of the commercial representation in the province of Lapland, I am compelled to inform you that no effective measures have so far been taken by Finland for an honest solution of this problem.

The Ministry for Foreign Affairs of the Republic of Finland, in its notes Nos. 26400 and 26241, of November 20 and 21, instead of satisfying the indispensable conditions—presented in the USSR plenipotentiary's note of November 2, 1940—of the representation, has proceeded to create new difficulties. In its note of November 21 the Ministry for Foreign Affairs reported, that officials of the Petsamo consulate and of the subsection of the commercial representation are forbidden to travel to Liinahamari Harbor, Trifona Bay, and the Inari district, and that travel northward may take place only along highway No. 4.

I venture to draw Your Excellency's attention to the fact that Liinahamari Harbor, Trifona Bay, and the Inari district belong wholly within the province of Lapland, and therefore also within the consular district of the Petsamo consulate of the USSR, which the Ministry for Foreign Affairs in its Note No. 21262 of August 2, 1940, has recognized. Consequently the notification given by the Ministry for Foreign Affairs, prohibiting travel by officials of the consulate to these localities, is to be regarded as a new restriction intended to hinder the activities of the USSR Petsamo consulate, which is in conformity with neither the letter nor the spirit of Article 5 of the Peace Treaty concluded between the USSR and Finland on March 12, 1940, which article provides for the opening of a USSR consulate in Petsamo. Instead of settling the matter justly and speedily, the Ministry for Foreign Affairs refers to formal and other matters with the intention of defending the behavior of the police and military authorities, and of delaying the granting of the right of free travel within the province of Lapland.

The system of arbitrary police power, directed against the officials of the Petsamo consulate, to which I have called your attention in conversations and notes of the plenipotentiary representation, still continues, and in its notes of reply to the plenipotentiary representation, the Ministry for Foreign Affairs lends its support to the system.

In notifying you of the above, I have the honor to request Your Excellency to undertake speedy and effective measures, in order that arrangements be made for the right of travel of the officials of the USSR consulate and subsection of the commercial representation in Petsamo, and to settle the demands presented in Note No. 63 of November 2, 1940, of the plenipotentiary representation, which demands represent indispensable minimum conditions.

Accept, Your Excellency, my assurances of my deepest regard.

I. Zotov

Document 53

Telegram from the Ministry for Foreign Affairs to the Moscow Legation, December 11, 1940

In answer to Commissar Molotov, we have planned the following: As far as we know, Foreign Minister Günther has not stated to Madame Kollontay what Molotov declares he has, but said on November 27 that on the initiative of Sweden, and wholly in a tentative fashion, the question has been raised of a closer co-operation between Sweden and Finland on the basis of a common defensive and foreign policy. Minister Wasastjerna told Madame Kollontay on December 2 that the possibilities of a neutralization of Finland and Sweden were being studied. This does not mean that Stockholm would direct Finland's foreign policy. Finland's commitments in the field of foreign policy will not be abandoned in the slightest degree; the possible closer co-operation with Sweden means working on the basis created by this very treaty, the Peace of Moscow. We emphasize that the first condition for Finnish-Swedish co-operation in foreign affairs is, as far as we are concerned, the permanence of existing boundaries. Minister Günther's statement to Madame Kollontay proves that in Sweden also there is no inclination to arrange matters secretly, but to keep the Soviet Union informed.

Document 54

Telegram from the Ministry for Foreign Affairs to the Finnish Legation in Moscow, December 14, 1940

It is hoped that you will give your reply in accordance with our telegram (see Document 53), after you have consulted with Minister Assarsson, who, according to information from Minister Wasastjerna, has received directives today.

Document 55

Memorandum of the Commissariat for Foreign Affairs to the Finnish Legation in Moscow, on December 18, 1940

According to Article 7 of the Peace Treaty concluded by the USSR and Finland on March 12, 1940, each Contracting Party shall construct on its own territory and as far as possible during the year 1940, a railroad which connects Kandalaksha with Kemijärvi. Having undertaken this obligation, the USSR began to carry it out without delay, and constructed in the course of 1940 on its own territory from Kandalaksha to the Soviet-Finnish border. Finland on the other hand has not built in its territory a single kilometer of the Kandalaksha-Kemijärvi railroad, and thus has not carried out the obligation assumed in the Peace Treaty.

The Commissariat for Foreign Affairs calls the attention of the Finnish Government to this matter, and demands that the building of the Kandalaksha-Kemijärvi railroad in Finnish territory be completed in the shortest possible time.

Document 56

Telegram from the Finnish Legation in Moscow to the Ministry for Foreign Affairs, December 18, 1940

On the 18th of this month, I was unexpectedly called to the Kremlin by Molotov, before the second conversation with Assarsson. He said that he had expected a reply from me to his communication, but instead Envoy Assarsson had called on him about the matter. M. Molotov asked whether Finland's foreign policy had already been subordinated to Stockholm. I explained the matter according to your telegram (see Document 53). The conversation lasted 40 minutes, and in the course of the discussion I explained the question more fully, parallel with what Minister Assarsson had stated. M. Molotov said that the USSR Government adheres to its communication of December 6. It holds the view that a military or defensive alliance is involved, concerning which the USSR stated its view in the spring. He stated that it is we who are trying to introduce a new element into the status quo which the USSR wants to retain. Finland would not have the right to negotiate even with the USSR without Sweden's consent. Finland would thus be a vassal. Regarding Minister Assarsson's statement that Germany presumably would not object, although this had not yet been ascertained, Molotov said that apparently the ground had been sounded in Berlin. I replied that I knew nothing about the question. Molotov made a passing remark that it is equally important to know what Great Britain and the U.S.A. think, in which I concurred. In spite of my explanations, Molotov in closing repeated that the USSR Government adhered to its communication of December 6. It embodies the USSR standpoint and is a warning to the Finnish Government.

PAASIKIVI

Document 57

Telegram from the Moscow Legation to the Ministry for Foreign Affairs, on December 19, 1940

When I said, in the conversation on December 18, that the peace treaty has already been fulfilled, Commissar Molotov answered: "There are still many clauses unfulfilled." To my question which these clauses were, he replied: "For instance, the Kemijärvi Railway on which hardly any work has been done so far." I protested, whereupon he said: "Get it ready by next February." I said that that was impossible, and promised him information on the subject. On the same evening, December 18, Assistant Commissar for Foreign Affairs Vyshinski asked me to see him and presented a memorandum in which it was declared that the USSR has fulfilled its obligation under the Peace Treaty by constructing the railway on its own territory, while Finland has not built a single kilometer of the railway and has thus not fulfilled her duty in accordance with the Peace Treaty. The Commissariat demanded the completion of the railway in the briefest possible time. I emphasized the difficulty of the work, and that to my knowledge work on the railway was proceeding energetically. I asked the source of their information. He answered it had been furnished by the Ministry for Foreign Affairs to Zotov. I promised to give him information without delay. Mr. Vyshinski wanted to know approximately when the railway will be completed. I request the latest information, and that work shall proceed with the greatest possible energy. I ought to be able to state that the railroad will be completed next spring.

PAASIKIVI

Document 58

Note No. 27730 of M. Witting, Finnish Minister of Foreign Affairs, to M. Zotov, Soviet Envoy in Helsinki, December 21, 1940

EXCELLENCY:

In reply to your note No. 77, dated December 10, 1940, I have the honor to state the following:

In your proposals requesting the easing of travel regulations in the case of the USSR consular and commercial staff members in Petsamo, you base the granting of unlimited freedom of movement, in the Province of Lapland, upon the grounds that the Government of Finland has recognized, as the district of the USSR consulate in Petsamo, the whole Lapland Province.

I cannot, however, share your conception that the district within which the consulate functions is in itself an area within whose limits the officers of the consulate can travel without any restrictions. I refer to the fact, fully recognized in international relations, that diplomatic representatives must observe the laws of the country in which they serve, and that they are bound by existing police and other regulations. This applies especially to consular representatives, who lack the special rights and immunities of diplomats. Consular representatives must therefore conform, even in the Province of Lapland, to the restrictions upon travel which it is essential, in the interest of order and security, to maintain in the province.

Article 6 of the Peace Treaty provides that the USSR shall have the right to establish a consulate in Petsamo. It also provides that nationals of the USSR have the right to travel, through the Petsamo area, to and from Norway. The consulate in Petsamo is naturally to be compared with other consulates in the same area; its rights by no means include the right to more extensive freedom of travel than is provided by general regulations regarding travel, and by Article 6 of the Peace Treaty. At present, however, the staff of the Petsamo consulate and the staff of the commercial section enjoy the privilege of free travel everywhere in the Petsamo region, as is shown by note No. 27442 of the Foreign Ministry, dated the 13th of this month, which contains a notification of the lapsing of the special measures pertaining to Liinahamari and Trifona.

As regards travel in the Lapland Province, there are some parishes in the province to which travel without special permits is forbidden. The areas in question are indicated on the enclosed map; their limits are shown in red. The areas indicated in blue require, for travel, only personal identification cards. The Ministry for Foreign Affairs has desired, however, to go as far as possible in easing the travel of representatives of the USSR representatives in the prohibited areas. The measures in question were given in the note of the Ministry for Foreign Affairs on November 21, last.

In view of the fact that you, Mr. Minister, consider that this arrangement is not satisfactory to you, I ask you to note that no mere formal requirements, or measures that stem from the arbitrariness of Finnish authorities, are involved, as you seem to assume in your letter. What is involved is restrictions necessary for maintaining order and security, similar to those which obtain at the present time in most countries. Finnish authorities have done their best in granting advantages to the representatives of the USSR, within the limits of these general regulations, which greatly facilitate travel to and from the offices in Petsamo.

I would also like to mention that the representatives of no other country in Finland have requested that travel regulations be eased, nor have any such modifications been granted.

Accept, Your Excellency, my assurances of deepest respect.

ROLF WITTING

Document 59

Note No. 20161 of the Ministry for Foreign Affairs to the USSR Legation, on January 4, 1941

Reference to the conversation between Minister for Foreign Affairs Witting and Minister Zotov, concerning the freedom of travel of officials of the USSR consulate in Petsamo, in the course of which Zotov expressed the view that the freedom of movement of the consular officials should extend, as applying to Petsamo, also to Inari Lapland, thus primarily the Inari and Utsjoki communes, the Ministry for Foreign Affairs has the honor to present the following explanation of what the term Petsamo area means.

Originally the "Petsamo area" comprised no more than the area belonging to the Petsamo village community, in other words the area between the Arctic coast and the Petsamo mountains. That is to say, in the area which became a part of Finland under the terms of the Tartu Peace Treaty of 1920, there were three village communities: Petsamo, Paatsjoki, and Suonijoki, each of which constituted an administrative and economic unit. Historically, therefore, the term Petsamo area denoted only the Petsamo village community and lands in the Petsamo River region.

Later, however, the term "Petsamo area" began to be applied to the whole area attached to Finland under the terms of the Tartu Peace Treaty and bounded by the Arctic Ocean, South Varanger on the Norwegian side, the rural communes of Inari, Sodankylä and Savukoski, and in the east by the Kola peninsula. This area, the boundary of which toward the rest of Finland is the old political frontier, was called for a while in 1921, in accordance with a proclamation of January 21, 1921, the Petsamo Province. As such, it was subject to special regulations up to the end of that year. Since then, the area in question has remained a distinct area from an administrative, judicial and also ecclesiastical point of view, with precisely defined limits. From an administrative point of view, the Petsamo area thus defined constitutes a single rural commune, and this is of special importance in the present case—a single police or sheriff district. Judicially the Petsamo area forms a single district, and ecclesiastically the area constitutes a clearly defined single Lutheran parish. Even in the widest sense of the term, the Petsamo area thus constitutes a whole which is altogether distinct from Inari Lapland and Salla Lapland.

This explanation shows that the conception of the Petsamo area as also including, in respect to matters now under consideration, certain parts of Finnish Lapland, does not correspond to the conception which has long been valid in Finland, and has been expressed in administrative arrangement of the Petsamo area as a single area with exactly defined boundaries.

Document 60

Telegram from the Moscow Legation to the Ministry for Foreign Affairs, on January 15, 1941

Commissar Vyshinski invited me to call on him on January 14 in connection with the nickel affair. He said they demand an answer, for their patience is at an end. He again hinted that if no result could be achieved by friendly means, they would find ways to settle the matter. I answered in conformity with your telegram, in the same terms as Minister Witting to Minister Zotov. Vyshinski asked whether the matter depended on British consent. If that is the case, the Finnish Government should have cleared up the matter with Great Britain before negotiations were begun here, for they are useless if Great Britain does not consent. I said that we had made a proposal. If the USSR had approved it, the matter would have been settled. Vyshinski replied that it is impossible to accept our proposal. He demanded full clarity without delay. The USSR takes the view that our government does not wish to arrange the matter but prolongs it on all kinds of pretexts. If we wish it, they will come to Helsinki to negotiate. He emphasized that the USSR regards the matter as very important. My own view is that the negotiations must soon be continued either here or in Helsinki and statement made as soon as possible as to when we are ready to begin. I await your telegram. Rush.

PAASIKIVI

Document 61

Telegram from the Moscow Legation to the Ministry for Foreign Affairs, on January 21, 1941

Vyshinski invited me to see him on January 21 and desired an answer. I explained as per your telegram. Vyshinski, who was very abrupt, said that he did not wish to hear such explanations and pretexts. He regarded the answers of the Finnish Government to date as unsatisfactory. The Soviet Government no longer permits further delay or consents to postponement. He demanded a final answer not later than the day after tomorrow, January 23. If we do not give it he will inform the Soviet Government that the Finnish Government refuses. My explanations were of no avail. Of Ramsay's journey to England he said mockingly: "Perhaps you will send him right round the world, all the way to America." He again made a passing remark that the USSR has given Petsamo to Finland. My own view is that the least we can do the day after tomorrow is to inform them that we are ready to continue negotiations at once, either here or in Helsinki.

PAASIKIVI

Document 62

Note No. 21080 of the Ministry for Foreign Affairs to the USSR Legation, on January 24, 1941

In its note verbal No. 26421 of November 21 last, and the personal note of the Minister for Foreign Affairs, dated December 21 last, the Ministry for Foreign Affairs has brought to the knowledge of the USSR Legation the principle of the standpoint of the Finnish Government regarding the application of travel regulations to the personnel of the offices of foreign representatives in this country, and also the practical methods by which it has been found possible, without infringing on the principles involved, to alleviate, in accordance with wishes expressed by the Legation, the positon of USSR representatives in this particular respect. The Legation has, nevertheless, subsequently returned to the subject on several occasions, expressing dissatisfaction with the arrangements made and even accusing the Finnish authorities, whose official duty it is to apply the travel restrictions and to control their proper observance, of arbitrary behavior. Thus, for instance, Secretary of the Legation Shumilov, in the course of a call on Counsellor of Legation Nyyssönen on the 9th of this month, presented a new list of persons for whom he requested the three-month travel permits referred to in the afore-mentioned notes. The latest occasion was on the 15th of this month, when Minister Zotov took up the matter with the Minister for Foreign Affairs, M. Witting.

In this connection the Ministry finds it necessary to establish once again, that the standpoint of the Finnish Government, in regard to principle, based on rules generally accepted in international usage, is that the regulations now in force in Finland governing exceptional travel restrictions, apply also to the personnel of Foreign Office representatives. With the exception of the USSR Legation, no complaints have been made by representatives of any Power against this standpoint of the Finnish Government; these representatives have, in each specific case, applied whenever necessary for the prescribed permit.

On the other hand, persons serving in the offices of the USSR representatives have failed, on numerous specific cases, to observe the regulations in question, and the repeated proposals by the Legation make it appear that the Legation for its part does not regard the Finnish Government's principle as acceptable. For this reason, the Ministry for Foreign Affairs is compelled to state that in the view of the Ministry, the Legation's proposals unfortunately go beyond what can be regarded, in the light of international custom, as reasonable.

The circumstance that the district of the Petsamo consulate has been so defined as to include the Province of Lapland in its entirety does not, as the Ministry has pointed out to the Legation on several occasions, presuppose unlimited freedom of travel everywhere in that province, for it includes areas in which, under Finnish domestic laws, movement without special permit is prohibited. The approval of a given consular territory defines the territorial limits within which the consulate in question may carry out its official duties, but does not by any means free its personnel from the obligation to obtain the travel permit prescribed whenever this obligation is imposed by the regulations in force in regard to specific areas within the consular territory. On the other hand, there is no reason to assume that the permit required would be refused, in individual cases, to any member of the USSR consulate in Petsamo should his presence in a locality subjected to special travel restrictions belonging to the consular territory be necessary for reasons of official duty. It is natural that, as the Ministry has pointed out to the Legation on previous occasions in this connection, the Finnish authorities should do their best when requests for travel permits are submitted, to facilitate, in each individual case, the transaction of official business in Finnish territory by USSR representatives.

With reference to the above, the Ministry for Foreign Affairs has the honor to state that the easing of the travel restrictions of a general character for the personnel of the USSR offices cannot, in the present state of affairs, be expanded beyond what has previously been brought to the knowledge of the Legation. Awaiting action on the part of the Legation in order that the three-month travel permits, which it has been decided will be furnished to persons belonging to USSR offices, can be made out, the Ministry wishes to point out that lists of the persons in question were drawn up on the basis of a conversation between the Ministry and representatives of the Legation. In the course of the conversation, the representative of the USSR was informed of the refusal of the Ministry to grant permits to certain members of the USSR Legation, and of grounds for the refusal. In no event is it justifiable to claim, as one of the memoranda of the Legation claims, that the Ministry has "arbitrarily" limited the number of persons to whom permits should be granted.

In view of the additional wishes in this matter, which the Legation presented later, the Ministry regrets to say that the new list of persons again includes certain persons against whose obtaining of permits the Ministry has presented weighty reasons.

Document 63

Telegram from the Moscow Legation to the Ministry for Foreign Affairs, on February 6, 1941

The meeting on February 5 lasted 10 minutes. We stated that we agree to the mixed company demanded by the USSR provided that they agree to our demands regarding the majority of the stock and management. We promised our written proposal for the forenoon of the sixth. M. Krutikov replied that the question concerning a majority of the stock could be discussed, but he stated that our demand regarding management, which he called an ultimatum, is unreasonable and cannot be discussed. Because we did not want to force the issue further until they have become familiar with the written proposal, we suggested discussions on the sixth. They agreed to this. We fear that they will not give in on the management question. If we stick to our stand, negotiations may possibly be broken off. We negotiators feel that no retreat should take place on the management question, in connection with the economic agreement, for it involves, in fact, the Russification of the area.

PAASIKIVI

Document 64

Telegram from the Moscow Legation to the Ministry for Foreign Affairs, on February 11, 1941

In the meeting on February 11, we stated that we have taken preliminary measures to speed the matter. We promised that the mixed company will be founded and the mine taken over within a week of ratification. As regards the problem of compensation, we agreed to accept the solution proposed by an expert outside party, in case we do not reach an agreement as to price, which still is to be disclosed. We accepted the Russian proposal that the property shall be turned over to the mixed company unencumbered, except for the claims of the I.A. Farbenindustrie, if the I.A. Farbenindustrie does not agree to the change. We stated that we cannot retreat in the management matter. We promised that if the management question is solved, we would ask for new instructions concerning the power works and the division of stock. In our view, we have now gone to the utmost limit. After he had advised us to ask for new instructions, to which we did not reply because he explained, in the same breath, that Russia would bargain about nothing, M. Krutinov noted that the committee's work has produced no results. He would communicate this to his government. The meeting lasted 40 minutes. We await your instructions.

FIEANDT

Document 65

Telegram from the Moscow Legation to the Ministry for Foreign Affairs, on February 13, 1941

Commissar Vyshinski asked me to call on him on February 12 concerning the nickel problem. I said that I had no more by way of instructions than our negotiations, and that I spoke only for myself. He stated several times that they have no ulterior motives, that their objective is economic, but that they want equality and the organization of production in the most efficient manner because they will invest much capital in the company. We went through the questions in dispute. The time for enacting the necessary legislation which has been shortened to three months he considered too long. A month should be enough. I said that we shall arrange the matter in the shortest possible time and that in my belief the time could still be somewhat shortened. In the board of the company, Vyshinski proposed parity, and an alternating chairman. The basis for this was, among other things, that the USSR is a Great Power and Finland a small country, so that even the prestige of the USSR demands equality. My remark that Britain had considered the matter in a different way had no effect. He clung to the demand for one-fifth of the technicians, foremen and office personnel. He knew that the negotiations had mentioned a fifty-fifty arrangement regarding the stock and the power station. A lengthy discussion developed on the question of the post of manager. M. Vyshinski demanded a Soviet manager because some sort of equality and equilibrium is essential. Finland has the territory, political power, and the apparatus of the business. I remarked, *inter alia,* about the sovereignty of Finland. He replied that there is no question of violating our sovereignty. Regarding the post of managing director, I stuck to our position. M. Vyshinski, who was friendly during the conversation that lasted an hour, said that the Government of the USSR demands the post of director and asked me to inform the government to that effect.

PAASIKIVI

Document 66

Telegram from the Moscow Legation to the Ministry for Foreign Affairs, February 19, 1941

In the discussion with M. Vyshinski on the 12th of this month I said jokingly: "The post of managing director is too small a matter for you to begin a war against us on that score." M. Vyshinski replied: "We are already engaged in a commercial war with each other."

PAASIKIVI

Document 67

Telegram from the Moscow Legation to the Ministry for Foreign Affairs, February 19, 1941

While calling on Vyshinski on the 18th of this month I stated that our government considers it natural that the management of the company and of the business should remain in our hands. The detailed arrangements regarding the nickel problem will best be negotiated in the Mixed Committee. I added to the bases of our stand. M. Vyshinski very curt from the start. He said that my reply thus is in the negative. He stated that the USSR is a Great Power and has an interest in the nickel. Finland would have the whole apparatus. He did not want to repeat what he had stated before. The proposals of the USSR are categorical, and the Soviet will not abandon them. He will inform his government of my reply, and there is no reason for continuing the work of the Mixed Committee. He said that there is thus nothing that can be done, and that the matter will now take its course, with all its consequences. He held that the purpose of Finland's reply was to prolong the question. I denied this and observed that the Mixed Committee handles all the questions. He answered by saying that the Government of the USSR has taken up, through him, the diplomatic-political questions which have not been solved in the Mixed Committee. As he has not been given a clear answer to them, he considers it an insult and protests. He closed the discussion abruptly and was angrier than ever before.

PAASIKIVI

Document 68

Telegram from the Moscow Legation to the Ministry for Foreign Affairs, March 5, 1941

Commissar Molotov called me to the Kremlin on March 4. He regretted that no conclusion had yet been reached by Finland and the USSR. I answered that it was they who had discontinued the negotiations of the Mixed Committee. Mentioning also the illness of M. Krutikov, he said that the solution of some questions by the two governments—such as the post of managing director, the number of members on the board of directors, the number of shares and one-fifth of the officers—is a prerequisite of the negotiations. I said that I had no instructions other than those I had presented to M. Vyshinski on February 18. I remarked that the chairman of the Finnish delegation, M.

Fieandt, is still here. We have made great concessions (I enumerated them) and we now expect them to agree. M. Molotov said that they made the greatest concession by giving Petsamo to Finland, for which there was no compelling reason when peace was made in 1920 and in 1940. He advised Finland to remember this and wondered that Finland is unwilling to arrange the matter, but has dragged it on for months. He emphasized several times that they demand the post of managing director because they want to make sure that the mining operations are efficiently conducted, and because they have experienced men. They have none but economic objectives. I answered that it is to our interest also that mining be efficient, and that we have experienced specialists. The mines are in Finnish territory, and therefore the management belongs to us. A lengthy discussion ensued regarding this. M. Molotov said, among other things, that the post of chairman of the board of directors can be discussed, but not the post of managing director. He asked for the final reply of the Government of Finland at the earliest opportunity. I promised to inform the government and to come back to the question. No secretary attended the discussion. M. Molotov was cordial but very resolute.

PAASIKIVI

Document 69

Telegram from the Ministry for Foreign Affairs to the Moscow Legation, May 8, 1941

On May 5 the Foreign Minister, M. Witting, had a general discussion with M. Orlov. M. Witting gave M. Orlov to understand that in our view the USSR has presented, after the Moscow peace which was supposed to have satisfied the USSR, additional demands such as those relative to transit traffic to Hanko, Aaland, nickel, and has not carried out the promise to ship grain which is in accordance with the commercial treaty. These things create a psychologically unfavorable effect here. We do not know what question may come up after the nickel problem, which therefore has to be judged against this background. The nickel question can most easily and most speedily be arranged as an economic question, on the basis of the present setup; that is, without changing the situation as regards the concession or ownership. We do not, however, want to retreat from the position we took in the meetings of the Mixed Committee in Moscow. We are ready to continue negotiations even on that basis and suggest that they be carried on in Helsinki. But it is our hope that the USSR would once more consider abandoning the idea of a mixed mining company, for that would have a psychologically beneficial effect at this time. Our Chargé d'Affaires in Moscow will soon present our reply.

Document 70

Telegram from the Moscow Legation to the Ministry for Foreign Affairs, May 11, 1941

On May 10, I presented your stand in the nickel question to M. Vyshinski, Assistant Commissar for Foreign Affairs, in accordance with your letter No. 3325 and your telegram. He listened without interrupting, and said that the matter was at the point reached three months ago, and that he considered himself able to say in advance that the reply does not satisfy [4] the USSR Government, and that discussion on the basis of the reply cannot be begun. He asked if a Soviet managing director violates Finland's sovereignty. I replied in the negative, but that Finland's Government considers it important that sovereignty be expressed in the composition of the directing organs of the company. M. Vyshinski promised to forward my communication to his government, and requested a written confirmation of it, which I promised to give.

HYNNINEN

Document 71

Envoy Hynninen's Written Reply to Commissar Vyshinski, May 10, 1941

The Government of Finland desires to call the attention of the Government of the USSR, in the Petsamo nickel question, to the following:

Although the Government of Finland has no kind of treaty obligation in this matter, it has shown good-will attitude toward the USSR and assumed a favorable attitude toward the wishes expressed by the Government of the USSR regarding this question. The Government of Finland has, for its part, desired in this way to improve the economic relations between the two countries, which it highly values.

In keeping with the wish expressed by the Government of the USSR some time ago, the Government of Finland stated that it stood ready to turn over to the USSR a substantial part of the production of the Petsamo mine. And the USSR having explained that it also desired to participate in the management and supervision of the mine, the Government of Finland formulated a new proposal. It was suggested that mining operations should remain in the hands of the present holder of the right to operate the mine, but that the distribution and sale of the product of the mine be given to a new Finnish-Russian company. When the USSR did not accept this alternative proposal, the Government of Finland, showing its good will, stated that it would agree to USSR participation in mining operations also.

In this connection, Finland's Government has held, and still holds, that the

---

[4] According to the later, written statement received from Envoy Hynninen, M. Vyshinski stated that Finland's reply "cannot be approved."

sovereign rights be given appropriate expression in the composition of the mixed company and its directive organs.

The proposal that the USSR should appoint the managing director of the company, cannot therefore be considered acceptable. The interests of the USSR in the company will be fully safeguarded by having its representative on the board of directors, which functions under the chairmanship of a Finnish chairman, and by having the same number of auditors as Finland. From the viewpoint of the company's functioning, it is an advantage that, with due regard to technical competence, the managing director should be a Finnish citizen familiar with conditions and a master of the languages of the country. It is in the interest of both countries that an efficient production program be maintained; it includes among other things deliveries to Germany, contemplated by contracts that bind even the Government of Finland. It is of course clear that proposals by the USSR which aim at increasing the efficiency of production, will in any case be acted upon by the Finns.

In designating the personnel of the company, the procedure can be that an agreement is formulated beforehand as to which of the two posts, previously promised to the USSR, shall be reserved to the Soviet Union, but the technical and local management will be kept in Finnish hands.

The Finnish Government stands ready to continue negotiations, on these bases, in the mixed committee, which it hopes will meet, on the basis of reciprocity, in Helsinki. But the Finnish Government would at the same time be pleased to have the matter arranged, as Finland's Foreign Minister has proposed to the USSR Envoy in Helsinki, by means of a commercial contract. This would mean a speedy solution, without any special legislation, all of which would create a particularly favorable impression in Finland and would smooth the way for better understanding between the two countries.

Document 72

Memorandum Presented by the Commissariat for Foreign Affairs to the Moscow Legation, on May 13, 1941

After acquainting itself with the memorandum presented by the Finnish Minister in Moscow, M. Paasikivi, on November 1, 1940, to the USSR Commissar for Foreign Affairs, V. M. Molotov, and the draft treaty relating to the flow of the Vuoksi River and the building of the Enso power station, the Commissariat for Foreign Affairs has the honor to state the following: The draft agreement relating to the regulation of the flow of the Vuoksi River and the building of the Enso power station, handed by the Commissariat for Foreign Trade to the Finnish Legation in Moscow on August 16, 1940, was drafted wholly in accordance with Article 2 of the Peace Treaty concluded between the USSR and

Finland on March 12, 1940, and with Article 6 of the protocol appended to the said treaty. It is also in keeping with international usage.

The USSR possesses an indisputable right, under the terms of the Peace Treaty, to carry to a conclusion the building of the Enso water power station situated in the territory ceded to the USSR, and in that connection to raise the level of the Vuoksi in conformity with the technical plans drafted in Finland for the Enso water power station.

The demands brought forward on behalf of Finland for the supply, by the USSR, of 300 million kilowatt hours annually as compensation for the loss by Finland of potential water power which Finland would be able to utilize if an electrical power station (Vallinkoski) were built in Finnish territory, are unfounded.

As regards the Finnish reference to international law, there is no rule in international law which assumes the payment of compensation for the exploitation of the potential water power of a river flowing from the territory of one state to the territory of another state. The Geneva Convention of December 9, 1923, which regulates in detail the relations of the respective states in regard also to the exploitation of water power, does not either contain any such rule.

On the other hand, Article 3 of the USSR draft agreement provides, in accordance with international usage, for the partial indemnification of the Finnish Government for damage caused the Finnish Government by the flooding of lands in Finnish territory in connection with the construction of the Enso power station dam in the Vuoksi River. The amount of this indemnification shall be approved in a special agreement between the governments of the two parties to the agreement.

The demand presented by Finland for the payment of compensation to the Enso-Gutzeit Company for costs incurred in connection with the drafting of the plans, the specifications of machinery ordered, and work on the drafting of contracts, is unfounded, for the terms of the peace treaty do not provide for compensation for property transferred to the USSR, and the USSR has not undertaken responsibility for obligations entered into by individuals or corporations in respect of property ceded to the USSR. For these reasons, and because of the new contracts entered into by economic organizations in the USSR and contractors for machinery, the USSR cannot undertake to pay to the Enso-Gutzeit Company the advance payments made by it to its own contractors.

The USSR takes notice of the consent by Finland to the proposal embodied in Article 5 of the USSR draft agreement, regarding the transfer to the construction company of the Enso water power station of certain contracts concluded by the Enso-Gutzeit Company with machinery contractors which may be useful for the completion of the construction of this water power station. On these grounds the USSR adheres to its proposal that the basis for an agreement shall be the USSR draft agreement presented to the Finnish Legation on August 16, 1940.

Document 73

Notes on Conversations between the Minister for Foreign Affairs, M. Witting, and the Soviet Envoy, M. Orlov, on June 21-23, 1941

On June 21, Minister Witting told M. Orlov that the Finnish Government had heard rumors of larger Soviet troop concentrations on the Finnish frontier than usual, and asked, referring to current rumors, whether war would break out between Germany and the USSR. Orlov gave assurances that there was not even a likelihood that war would break out. On June 22 Witting observed, in a conversation with Orlov in the evening, that a state of war existed between Germany and the USSR. M. Witting enumerated the bombardments of Finland by USSR air and land forces, which had occurred that day (Alskar, two Finnish war vessels, a Finnish transport on the way to the Aaland Islands) and presented a protest. Orlov said he would not accept the protest and claimed, referring to Commissar Molotov's speech that day, that no such bombings had occurred, but that on the contrary flights had been made from Finland into Russia.

Witting replied that the 14 bombers which had naturally returned to the USSR from their bombing raid in Finland, had obviously come from the Finnish side and renewed his protest. Orlov then promised to look into the matter. He asked what Finland's attitude is in the conflict that had arisen. Minister Witting answered that Parliament would discuss the matter on June 25, and added that continued violations of Finnish territory would not improve the relations between Finland and the USSR.

On June 23, Minister Witting informed M. Orlov that in accordance with the Agreement of 1921 Finland had garrisoned the Aaland Islands, presented a protest with reference to fire opened by the Russians in the region of Lake Immola, and brought to Orlov's knowledge the request, made by the USSR consul in Mariehamn, M. Orlenko, to Governor Österberg for permission to move with his staff from the Aaland Islands to Helsinki.

Document 74

Excerpts from the Speech Broadcast by the President of the Republic, Risto Ryti, June 26, 1941

CITIZENS:

This peace-loving nation, which for more than a year has strained all its energies to the utmost, to reconstruct the country and bring it to a new state of prosperity after the ravages of the last war, has again become the victim of a brutal attack. Once again the same enemy, who has attacked this small country at brief intervals for 90 out of the past 500 years, ravaging, destroying and murdering, has invaded our territory with his air force, killing peaceful citizens, chiefly old people, women and children, and destroying the property of peaceful citizens.

Immediately after the outbreak of war between Germany and the Soviet Union four days ago, the integrity of our frontiers was violated on numerous occasions by the Soviet Union, in consequence of which we presented energetic protests, but without any result. Regardless of agreements and without any cause on our part, Soviet military forces have since yesterday carried out, at the order of their government, regular, extensive hostilities in all parts of the country and, as is their habit, have directed them chiefly against fully open localities and the peaceful civilian population.

Thus our second defensive struggle less than nineteen months after the first attack has begun. The new attack on Finland by the Soviet Union is the terminal point of the policy followed by the Soviet Union toward Finland since the Peace Treaty of Moscow in March 1940. The purpose of that policy has been to destroy the independence of our nation and to enslave our people.

After we had been left without military aid in our winter war of 1939–40, we were compelled, in the dark hours of the night on March 12, to conclude peace with the Soviet Union. That peace seemed paralyzingly severe after the successful defense we had made at the cost of heavy sacrifices. Already the peace terms were an indication of what the hidden purposes of the Soviet Union had been in dictating those terms. The new frontier was drawn up in a way that was to destroy once and for all Finland's possibilities of defense. The frontier was made to cut across all natural defensive lines and in such a way as to break up altogether the highway system of the country. By the Peace Treaty the Soviet Union procured for itself a new point of departure, favorable from the military point of view, for an eventual new war of aggression.

Nor was this enough. To render Finland wholly defenseless against attack by its enormous armed forces, the Soviet Union demanded the Hanko naval base, and the construction of the Salla railway. The reason put forward for the leasing of the Hanko base to the USSR was that the Soviet Union must obtain this key position on the Gulf of Finland to secure the safety of the great maritime city of Leningrad.

However, the armed forces stationed at Hanko are less suggestive of naval defense than of an attack, and an attack by land. For a naval battle one does not need large tank units or enormous railway guns. The force at Hanko has chiefly been put together with an eye to a swift attack by land. Hanko resembles a pistol aimed straight at the heart of Finland. Neither the demand for the construction of the Salla railway nor the territorial demands in regard to Northeast Finland were included in the preliminary peace terms communicated to the Finnish Government. The threat in this demand for a railway was directed at North Scandinavia in its entirety, but was in the first place a dagger aimed at Finland's back.

In connection with the peace negotiations it was stated, as the definite and absolute standpoint of the Soviet Union, that the agreement reached in March 1940 fully satisfied the demands of the Soviet Union. The Soviet delegates regarded the peace treaty as guaranteeing the safety of Leningrad, to secure which the Soviet Union explained that it had embarked on hostilities. Similarly, the Soviet delegates expressed their assurance that the treaty guaranteed the security of the Murmansk railway to the northeast of Lake Ladoga, a matter which the Soviet Union regarded as important from the point of view of its communications. Further, the delegates gave assurances that the manner in which Finland decided matters of domestic and foreign policy was wholly her own business, and also the manner in which she organized her economic affairs. The Soviet Union had no interest in them.

Although we Finns had our own painful experiences of how little an agreement concluded on behalf of the Soviet Union means, we did nevertheless expect that a word given would be kept at least to some extent, and at least for some period of time. But again we were soon to see that no word from Soviet Russian quarters can be trusted.

Regardless of promises not to interfere with Finland's foreign policy, the Soviet Union brought forward demands in regard to the direction of Finland's foreign policy. After the heavy battles fought and the serious losses sustained by us, and in the absence of protection from field defenses, this country was wholly unprotected against new attacks by the Soviet Union.

To secure existence of our country at least in some manner, the Finnish Government tried to open conversations with a view to bringing about a defensive alliance of the northern countries. These conversations were made public on the day on which peace was concluded in Moscow. When the Finnish Parliament, on March 21, was discussing the documents relating to the Peace Treaty, the Soviet Government presented in Moscow a strong protest against the project, declaring wholly without cause that it was in conflict with the Peace Treaty.

In connection with the same issue of foreign policy the Soviet Union interfered on three further occasions, in a threatening manner, in our right of self-determination: on September 27, 1940, Independence Day, December 6 last year, and about two weeks later, on December 18. This happened in spite of the fact that the idea of a defensive alliance was not in any way directed against anybody, but was merely intended for the protection of the three sister nations.

Contrary to all international custom and practice, the diplomatic and consular representatives of the Soviet Union in Finland have carried on interference in Finland's domestic affairs, and even espionage to the extent of using forged passports and assumed names. With this intention the corps of the Soviet personnel has been extraordinarily expanded. Attached to the Helsinki Legation were 31 persons belonging to the Diplomatic Corps, and 120 staff members. At the Petsamo consulate there were 3 consuls and 21 assistants, at the Mariehamn consulate 8 consuls and 30 other persons.

Altogether there have thus been, in the service of the Soviet personnel in Finland, 42 members of the diplomatic corps and 171 assistants. Utilizing both its Legation and some Finnish citizens, who have been willing to trade their Fatherland for thirty pieces of silver, the Soviet Union has unscrupulously striven to interfere in Finnish domestic affairs. By supporting and encouraging the subversive activities of the "Society for Friendship and Peace Between Finland and the Soviet Union," which was actually directed and aided from Moscow, the Soviet Union has tried to make Finland ripe for a development similar to that which it had succeeded in bringing about in the Baltic States.

The Soviet Union has even attempted to meddle in questions of domestic appointments. Soviet propaganda and espionage in Finland became ever more unscrupulous and active. Every Finn who has fallen into Soviet hands, beginning with prisoners of war, has been the object of attempts by inducement or compulsion to enlist him for espionage work in Finland.

Soviet propaganda has sown hate of the Finnish Government and public authorities. It has endeavored to spread Bolshevism and Bolshevist thought in Finland. The latest indication of the insolence which the Soviet Union continued to show in most varied ways is a proposal, presented quite recently from official Soviet quarters, that a certain person now serving the sentence pronounced on him for espionage in the biggest espionage case ever known in Finland, should be released and allowed to proceed to the Soviet Union.

Political and economic demands made by the Soviet Union, going far beyond those included in the Peace Treaty, extended to many different fields and became ever more serious from the point of view of the national security. I will mention a few of them.

On June 23 last year the Soviet Union sprang a surprise on us, by taking up the question of the Aaland Islands, which was not included in the peace terms. When, to repulse the new demand, we referred to this circumstance, Foreign Commissar Molotov cynically remarked that the Soviet Government had not taken up the question of the Aaland Islands in connection with the Peace Treaty as that might have had a disturbing effect on the peace negotiations. The Soviet Government now demanded that the Aaland Islands were to be demilitarized, the defense works there destroyed, and facilities given to the Soviet Union to control on its own behalf the work of demolition.

By these demands the Soviet Union clearly wished to reserve to itself an opportunity for an easy capture of the Aaland Islands at the appropriate moment. About the same time, or about a year ago, the Union presented demands in regard to the Petsamo nickel mines. The Soviet Union was not content to demand a part of the output of these mines: its demands were of a directly political character. The Soviet Union demanded that the management of the mines should be handed over to it, and *inter alia,* the right to appoint a fifth of the personnel of the mines. The placing of a body of men of that size in the Petsamo area would have meant that, in actual fact, the Soviet Union had acquired a military base in Petsamo also. It is illustrative of the double-dealing character of the Soviet, that the USSR reported the nature of its demands in regard to Petsamo nickel to us, and to interested Great Powers, in wholly different forms. One Power was informed that the Soviet Union has only an economic interest in Petsamo nickel; another was told that the question was a political measure directed at the Petsamo area.

A third disturbing demand concerned military transports by railway through Finnish territory to the leased Hanko area. These agreements, too, were not stipulated in the peace treaty. The dangerous nature of such transports from the point of view of the nation's security and right of self-determination was obvious. By these means the Soviet Union strove in different ways to weaken Finland's political and military position.

Meanwhile, the Soviet Union tried in every way to reduce our capacity for resistance by economic measures. Without the slightest foundation in the provisions of the Peace Treaty, it demanded the surrender of a considerable quantity of rolling stock. The Soviet Union also demanded compensation for property alleged to have been moved out of the ceded territory or destroyed, extending these demands to property moved out of the leased Hanko area, to which the Soviet Union could in no case have any claim. Illustrative of these demands is that compensation was demanded for certain machines which had been sold by Carelian industrial enterprises and transported away several years before the war broke out. Apparently, they had been included in lists drawn up earlier by Soviet spies, on which the claims for compensation were based.

Further, the Soviet Union demanded for itself the valuable Vallinkoski Rapids in the River Vuoksi, situated in its entirety in undisputed Finnish territory. The basis for this claim was that the Finns had earlier planned the linking of this water power establishment with the Ensonkoski Rapid, which had fallen within the territory ceded to Russia.

Thus, by continued pressure and repeated threats, the Soviet Union strove to improve its position, to extend its influence in Finland and to weaken our economic position which was difficult enough already. In numerous instances we were compelled to accede to the Soviet demands. In others, negotiations were proceeding when the new war broke out.

Accustomed to keep its word, the Finnish nation wished to honor the agreements we were compelled to conclude in Moscow. In our hearts we decided, and also declared on innumerable occasions, that we had to regain all that was lost in Carelia by domestic reforms and new productive work within our new frontiers. Calm deliberation brought us to that conclusion. The idea of revenge was not evident and has not influenced our policy. On the Finnish side we tried to forget the wrongs and humiliations inflicted on us, although the wounds struck by the Soviet Union's war of aggression, begun in defiance of all international justice and moral principles, burned in the hearts of the entire nation. The point from which we set out was, that seeing we had to live in this corner of the world, from generation to generation, in the immediate neighborhood of Russia, our relations with that country had to be organized. In spite of all that had happened, we wished to build up a lasting peace with the Soviet Union.

This will of ours to peace was subjected on more than one occasion to a strain, as can be seen from the incessant demands to which I have referred. To demonstrate our wish for peace and in the hope that, by submitting this once more to demands, we should at least prevent or at any rate postpone, the outbreak of an open conflict with the Soviet Union, and in some way permanently consolidate our relations, we showed great submission. Nor did we limit our efforts at creating good relations to passive submission. We developed an interest in the active stimulation of relations.

Attempts were made on our side to create reciprocal relations in the most various fields. For the creation and cultivation of cultural relations we founded a special society, "The Baltic Circle." In Soviet quarters, however, the initiatives taken by this society were repulsed, and the same applied to other initiatives in private quarters. The Soviet Union adopted the same attitude to official attempts at a rapprochement. The thorough proposals worked out by the official "Commission for the Promotion of Cultural Relations between Finland and the Soviet Union," appointed by the Ministry of Education, found no response in the Soviet Union, which did not even consent to receive the Finnish Minister of Education to discuss the development of cultural relations. Further, we have made the sincerest efforts, in spite of all difficulties, to develop trade relations.

The trend of Soviet activities toward us is clear from all that I have submitted to you. The independence of Finland was to be destroyed either with the aid of domestic upheavals and difficulties, or else by the forcible conquest of the country. When the path of domestic revolution was soon to be closed because of our nation's great love of liberty, and of our internal unity, the Soviet Union decided to take the path of violence.

With this in mind, M. Molotov, chief and foreign Commissar of the Soviet Union, demanded of Germany during the Berlin negotiations of November 12–13, 1940, or only seven months after the peace of Moscow, a free hand to strike a final blow at Finland and to liquidate us. . . .

Since the outbreak of the present Great War, the intentions and attitude of the Soviet Union have been clearly evident. The Soviet Union watched with satisfaction the outbreak of the conflict, and aimed all the time at extending and prolonging it as much as possible, in order that the European nations, and if possible, nations outside of Europe as well, might thereby be materially and morally weakened, their powers of resistance to Bolshevist agitation reduced, so that they would fall an easy prey to Soviet imperialism when in the opinion of the Soviet Union the appropriate moment for armed intervention in the war had come. The Soviet Union has ruthlessly exploited various situations, with the result that our country too was placed in a position in which, while the war between the Great Powers raged on other fronts, we had to meet unaided the immense superiority of the Soviet Union. We do not hate the longsuffering and oppressed peoples of the Soviet Union, but after all that has occurred, who would expect us to go into mourning if M. Molotov, and with him the circles responsible for Russia's policy, now have fallen victims to their own policy, which has been the policy of scavengers?

Now that the Soviet Union has extended hostilities to Finnish territory by attacking this peaceful nation, it is our duty to defend ourselves. We shall do so, determined and united, with all the moral and material means at our disposal.

Our hardened defense forces, as brave and as self-sacrificing but better armed and equipped than in the last war, take up the battle for the liberty of the fatherland, the "living space" of our people, the faith of our fathers and our free social order. In common with all those men and women who, at the fronts or on the home front, working at different duties, sacrifice with enthusiasm their energies and efforts for the benefit of our defense and the whole of our internally united nation, they are inspired at this decisive moment by the spirit of Comradeship in Arms born of our last war, and guided by a firm resolve to strive in increasing measure for the realization of greater justice in our body politic and social. Our confidence in our Army and in Field Marshal Mannerheim is absolute.

Citizens! The centuries have shown that in the corner of the world where Fate placed this nation, permanent peace cannot be achieved. The pressure of the East is always upon us. To reduce this pressure, to destroy the eternal menace, to secure a happy and peaceful life for coming generations, we now embark on our defensive battle. The Lord of Destiny, in whose hands lies the life of our nation, guides us and will carry our struggle to ultimate victory.

INDEX

Numbers refer to Documents

Aaland Islands
  Agreement between Finland and USSR concerning the, 34
  Consulate of the USSR in, 29, 34, 39, 45, 47, 73, 74
  Demilitarization of, 16, 25, 34, 39, 69, 74
  International Agreement of nonfortification and neutralization of, 25, 31, 73
  Obligation to Consult USSR in connection with, 30, 31
Alskär, island in the Aaland archipelago, 73
Archives, left in ceded territory, 25
Assarsson, Swedish Envoy to USSR, 54, 56

Baltic Circle, 74
Baltic Sea, 34
Baltic States, 74
Buschmann, Gerhard Arnold Wilhelm, 13

Cession of territory to USSR
  Archives left in ceded territory, 25
  Destruction of property in the ceded area after the conclusion of peace, 9, 11
  Restoration of property belonging to industrial establishments in the territory ceded to USSR, 8, 11, 74
  Scientific material relating to the ceded territory, 25
  Territory ceded in Northeast Finland, 74
Colliers, 43

Commission for promotion of cultural relations between Finland and USSR, 74
Cripps, Sir Stafford, British Ambassador to USSR, 37, 41, 42, 43

Dekanosov, Assistant Commissar for Foreign Affairs of USSR, 12

Enckell, Member of Finnish-Soviet Mixed Committee for investigation of property removed from Hanko, 35
Enso,
  Enso-Gutzeit Company, 24, 72
  Enso Power Plant, 11, 24, 36, 72
  Enso-Vallinkoski Rapids, 24, 36, 74
  Treaty for the Construction of the Enso Water Power Works, 24

Fieandt, Rainer von, former Minister of Supplies, 68
Fortifications on new border, 26

Gartz, 15, 16, 19
Geneva Convention of 1923 regarding exploitation of water power, 72
Gräsbeck, W., Chairman of Finnish-Soviet Mixed Committee for investigation of property removed from Hanko, 35
Günther, Minister for Foreign Affairs of Sweden, 1, 4, 50, 53
Gulf of Finland, 13, 74

Hambro, Speaker of the Norwegian Parliament, 3, 5, 6

Hanko,
  lease of Naval Base to USSR, 12, 17, 18, 25, 35, 74
  restoration of property in the Hanko Area, 10, 12, 17, 20, 21, 25, 35, 74
  transit agreement, 18, 23, 25, 69, 74
Helsinki-Tallin Air Line, 13
Hynninen, Finnish Minister to USSR, 70, 71

Imatra Power Plant, 36
Immola, 73
Inari, 47, 52, 59
Ivalo, 47

Jalanti, Assistant Division Chief of the Ministry for Foreign Affairs of Finland, 15, 19
Jelisejev, Counselor of the USSR Legation in Helsinki, 48

Kaleva, airplane, 13
Kemijärvi-Salla-Kandalaksha Railway, 49, 55, 57
Kivimäki, T. M., Finnish Envoy to Germany, 51
Koht, Minister for Foreign Affairs of Norway, 2
Kola Peninsula, 59
Kollontay, Madame, Soviet Minister to Sweden, 50, 53
Kotilainen, Minister of Trade and Industry, 15, 16, 19
Krutikov, 63, 64, 68

Lapland, Province of, 45, 52, 58, 62
Leningrad, 5, 74
Liinahamari, 47, 52, 58

Mannerheim, Field-Marshal, 51, 74
Molotov, Vjatsheslav Mihailovitsh, President of the Council of Commissars of the USSR and Commissar for Foreign Affairs, 5, 6, 14, 15, 16, 22, 23, 25, 26, 27, 28, 29, 30 31 33, 37, 40, 41, 42, 46, 50, 51, 53, 56, 57, 68, 72, 74

Murmansk Railway, 5, 74
Northern Defensive Alliance, 1, 2, 3, 4, 5, 7, 30, 50, 53, 54, 56, 74
Norway, 2, 3, 4, 5, 7

Orlov, P. D., Soviet Minister to Finland, 35, 69, 73
Österberg, Governor of the Aaland Islands, 73

Paasikivi, Juho Kusti, Finnish Envoy to the USSR, 5, 6, 8, 11, 12 14-16, 19, 22, 23, 26-34, 37, 40-42, 44, 46, 50, 51, 56, 57, 60, 61, 63, 65-68, 72
Petsamo,
  Attempts to gain control of the Petsamo Nickel Mines, 14, 15, 16, 19, 27, 30, 37, 38, 40, 41, 42, 43, 44, 46, 60, 61, 63, 64, 65, 66, 67, 68, 69, 70, 71, 74
  British-Canadian Mond Nickel Company, 15, 27
  Soviet Consulate in, 25, 39, 45, 47, 52, 58, 59, 62, 74
  Soviet commercial representation in, 45, 47, 52, 58, 59
  Travel of members of Soviet Consulate in, 39, 45, 47, 52, 58, 59, 62
Presidential Election in Finland, Soviet interference in, 51
Prisoners, Exchange of, 25

Ramsay, H., 61
Repatriation of Members of the Finnish Army and civilians, 25
Revolutionary activities supported by the USSR in Finland, 74
Ryti, Risto, President of the Republic of Finland, 25, 26, 38, 74

Saimaa, Lake, 24
Salla Railway, 25, 49, 55, 57, 74
Sandler, Richard, former Foreign Minister of Sweden, 5
Shumilov, Secretary of the Legation of the USSR in Finland, 62
Society for Peace and Friendship be-

tween Finland and the USSR, 22, 23, 26, 74
Stalin, 5, 16
Stepanov, USSR, Commissar for Foreign Trade, 36
Svinhufvud, 51
Sweden, 2, 3, 4, 5, 7, 28, 33

Tanner, Väinö, former Foreign Minister of Finland, 5, 22, 26, 51
Trade
 between Finland and the USSR in 1940-41, 16, 25, 69
 war on Finland, 66
Trifona Bay, 47, 52, 58

Vallinkoski Rapids, 36, 40, 72, 74
Vasilevski, Aleksander Mihailovitsh, Brigadier, 34
Vereker, British Envoy to Finland, 37, 42, 43

Viipuri, 21, 35
Voionmaa, Tapio, Secretary General for Foreign Affairs at Helsinki, 48
Voionmaa, Väinö, Professor, 5, 12
Vuoksi River, 24, 36, 72, 74
Vyshinski, Assistant Commissar for Foreign Affairs of USSR, 37, 38, 41, 42, 44, 46, 57, 60, 65, 66, 67, 68, 70, 71

Waris, P., Lieutenant-Colonel, 13
Wasastjerna, Finnish Envoy to Sweden, 50, 53, 54
Wickström, Member of Finnish-Soviet Mixed Committee for the investigation of property removed from Hanko, 35
Witting, Rolf, Minister for Foreign Affairs of Finland, 49, 52, 58, 59, 60, 62, 69, 73

Zotov, Soviet Envoy to Finland, 38, 48, 49, 52, 57, 58, 59, 60, 62

www.ingramcontent.com/pod-product-compliance
Lightning Source LLC
Chambersburg PA
CBHW050839160426
43192CB00011B/2087